# Dreams
Three works by

# Olive Schreiner

# Titles in this series

*Anna Lombard*
by Victoria Cross
Edited by Gail Cunningham

*Dreams, Visions and Realities*
An anthology of short stories by turn-of-the century women writers
Edited by Stephanie Forward, with a foreword by Ann Heilmann

*Keynotes* and *Discords*
by George Egerton
Edited by Sally Ledger

*The History of Sir Richard Calmady*
by Lucas Malet
Edited by Talia Schaffer

*The Creators*
by May Sinclair
Edited by Lyn Pykett

*Dreams*
by Olive Schreiner
Edited by Elisabeth Jay

**Late Victorian and Early Modernist Women Writers**
Series Editors
Marion Thain and Kelsey Thornton

# Dreams
Three works:
*Dreams*
*Dream Life and Real Life*
and
*Stories, Dreams and Allegories*

by
Olive Schreiner

Edited by
Elisabeth Jay

**THE UNIVERSITY
OF BIRMINGHAM**

UNIVERSITY PRESS

Introduction and apparatus Copyright © Elisabeth Jay 2003

Published in the United Kingdom by The University of Birmingham Press, Edgbaston, Birmingham, B15 2TT, UK.

All rights reserved. Except for the quotation of short passages for the purposes of criticism and review, no part of the work may be reproduced, stored in a retrieval system, or transmitted, in any form or by any means, electronic, mechanical, photocopying, recording or otherwise, without the prior permission of the publisher.

ISBN 1 902459 31 8

British Library Cataloguing in Publication Data

A CIP catalogue record for this book is available from the British Library

Printed in Great Britain by Lightning Source

# Contents

| | | |
|---|---|---|
| Series Editors' Introduction | | vii |
| Introduction by Elisabeth Jay | | ix |
| A Note on the Text | | xxix |

## DREAMS       1

| | | |
|---|---|---|
| I | The Lost Joy | 3 |
| II | The Hunter | 6 |
| III | The Gardens of Pleasure | 13 |
| IV | In a Far-Off World | 14 |
| V | Three Dreams in a Desert | 16 |
| VI | A Dream of Wild Bees | 22 |
| VII | In a Ruined Chapel | 25 |
| VIII | Life's Gifts | 29 |
| IX | The Artist's Secret | 30 |
| X | I Thought I Stood | 31 |
| XI | The Sunlight Lay Across My Bed | 33 |

## DREAM LIFE AND REAL LIFE       47

| | | |
|---|---|---|
| I | A Little African Story | 49 |
| II | The Woman's Rose | 56 |
| III | "The Policy In Favour of Protection—" | 59 |

## STORIES, DREAMS AND ALLEGORIES       65

| | |
|---|---|
| Preface by S. C. Cronwright-Schreiner | 67 |

### STORIES

| | |
|---|---|
| Eighteen-ninety-nine | 69 |
|     Nineteen hundred and one | 89 |
|     In the year nineteen hundred and four | 89 |
| The Buddhist Priest's Wife | 91 |
| On the Banks of a Full River | 100 |
| The Wax Doll and the Stepmother | 106 |
| The Adventures of Master Towser | 112 |

### DREAMS AND ALLEGORIES

| | |
|---|---|
| A Soul's Journey – Two Visions | 119 |
| God's Gifts to Men | 121 |

## Contents

| | |
|---|---|
| They Heard ... | 122 |
| Life's Gifts | 123 |
| The Flower and the Spirit | 124 |
| The River of Life | 125 |
| The Brown Flower | 126 |
| The Two Paths | 127 |
| A Dream of Prayer | 128 |
| Workers | 129 |
| The Cry of South Africa | 130 |
| Seeds A-Growing | 131 |
| The Great Heart of England | 133 |
| Who Knocks at the Door? | 134 |
| The Winged Butterfly | 138 |
| The Dawn of Civilisation | 139 |

**Glossary**     **145**

# Series Editors' Introduction

This series 'Late Victorian and Early Modernist Women Writers' owes its immediate inspiration to a casual grumble from Gail Cunningham. She was regretting that there are many splendid books by women at the turn of the nineteenth century which she would like to be able to teach, but that she was unable to put on her reading lists because her students would not be able to get hold of a copy. Anyone researching and teaching late Victorian and early modernist women writers will recognize this position: how difficult it can be to buy copies of prose texts which have changed the accepted view of literature of the period, and how frustrating that this revolution in the critical world cannot change the syllabuses we teach until good editions of these works are easily available. We decided to do something about it, and have designed a series which intends to bring back into print significant work by important and interesting women of the time, books which have been difficult to obtain but are nonetheless points of reference for those who study the period.

To establish a series of this sort is to make a clear statement about the changes taking place in our understanding of literary history and the place of women writers within it. It recognizes that a significant shift is being made in the way in which we must view not only the work produced in the late years of the nineteenth and the early years of the twentieth century but the critical position from which we understand it. We therefore thought it important to secure as editors critics and scholars whose work has figured significantly in assisting and defining this change.

Since one of the reasons for the neglect of these novels and stories is the nature of critical and social prejudices and opinions, we also thought that it was important to ask the editors to provide substantial contextualization, in introductions which should explain not only the importance of the writers for their own day but also for ours, and with substantial suggestions for further reading.

We trust that this group of books will enrich both courses in women's writing and courses on late Victorian and early modernist texts. The general reader too should find much to interest, amuse and entertain.

Marion Thain
Kelsey Thornton

# Introduction

For much of the twentieth century such reputation as Olive Schreiner enjoyed rested on her first published novel, *The Story of an African Farm* (1883) and upon the occasional testimonies to the influence of her polemical writing to be found in the more accessible work of a generation of pacifist women writing during and after the First World War. This positioned her as something of an oddity: a Victorian colonial whose work was largely remarkable either for having laid the foundations of South Africa's literary tradition, or having contributed to the development of a feminist analysis of a capitalist economy, but whose modest and somewhat naïve achievements could be assumed to have been assimilated or eclipsed by her successors.

This volume brings together for the first time the entire range of the shorter pieces of imaginative writing that she continued to produce throughout her life, together with her final account of the vision informing her life's work. It rescues Schreiner from the charge of having exhausted a slim talent in one semi autobiographical novel and provides a context in which to situate a woman writer whose idealist concerns recognised no simple geographical boundaries. To picture her as first and foremost a colonial writer or, alternatively, primarily as a member of the fin-de-siècle British avant garde, does little justice to the links she made in her own writing and to the complex situation she occupied, for Olive Emilie Albertina Schreiner's life (1855–1920) straddled two centuries and two continents, while her travels between the land of her birth, South Africa, and her family's European homeland embroiled her in the political ferment of two wars: the Boer War (1899–1902) and the first World War (1914–1918).

The mixed inheritance into which she was born as the sixth surviving child of the twelve sons and daughters of a German father and an English mother, themselves first-generation immigrants, combined with the peripatetic circumstances of this missionary household, provoked in her a strong need to wrestle with questions of identity. Never entirely at home in any of her successive abodes, fiercely guarding her independence but always searching for soul-mates, Schreiner did not settle exclusively upon any one genre in which to express her passionately held convictions about gender, religion, politics, social evolution and race. All who knew her remarked an intense physical restlessness, exacerbated by the search for a place or cause, which could provide the seemingly impossible combination of corporal, emotional and intellectual well-being she craved. Her refusal to identify herself wholly with any of the groups whose causes she espoused also contributed to the difficulty literary criticism has experienced in categorising her work.

The absence of an obvious school, tradition or movement to which to link her has proved as enticing to other disciplines as it has off-putting to literary scholarship. Historians, psychoanalytic critics and those variously anxious to co-opt her for English feminism or radical South African politics have all seized upon her work as virgin territory ripe for annexation. The metaphor is not accidental. The emergence of postcolonial studies has served to sensitise a new generation of readers to the particularity of the conditions under which the literature of the colonisers and the colonised was produced. Olive Schreiner has frequently been cited as South Africa's first major author, although, as her life story and the deliberate attribution of many of the tales in this collection to the European locations where they written will show, her relationship with the land of her birth was complex.

Schreiner's parents arrived in South Africa in 1838. Her father, Gottlob, was a German shoemaker turned Lutheran missionary, sent out under the auspices of the London Missionary Society. Although he lacked much formal education he was sufficient of a linguist to acquire English, Dutch and the Sotho language. Her mother, Rebecca Lyndall, was also from lower class origins. The daughter of a minister who had moved from the Wesleyan to the Calvinist wing of the Methodist connexion, Rebecca herself was to finish her days in a Roman Catholic convent. In the course of his twenty-seven years in the mission field Gottlob also changed his allegiance from Lutheran to Wesleyan before being expelled in 1865 for the misdemeanour of combining a little trading with his religious work. Schreiner's loss of orthodox faith consequent upon the death of a much-loved sister at 18 months, when she herself was only 10, has tended to obscure how much she was indebted to the religious environment of her upbringing. The mission-station homes of her childhood offered her a scant and random reading diet, but absorbing the rhythms of the Authorised King James Bible – her mother forbade the use of Dutch and Afrikans in the house – provided her with references, symbols, stories and rhetoric that would resonate equally for English speaking readers in South Africa and Europe.

Life in the colonies seemed to offer great potential for reshaping one's life by 'moving on' both geographically and ideologically. Taking up a trader's life, however, proved a transformation too far for Gottlob who went bankrupt within the year. The three youngest children: Ettie (17), Olive (12) and Will (10) were taken in by their brother Theo (23) – English educated like the other Schreiner boys – who had become a headmaster in the small South African township of Cradock. Schreiner's independent spirit, together with her desperate longing to find like-minded companions, were honed by spending her adolescence with the devoutly disapproving elder brother and sister. She was to experience none of the consolation that the Coventry band of freethinkers offered the rather older George Eliot in her 'holy war' with her family. This reduced family unit fell apart in 1870 when Theo and Will left to make their fortune at the Diamond Fields. Olive was passed around the homes of family and family friends in the hope that she would eventually earn her living as a governess. In this wider circle she met her first freethinker and gained access to some of the books that had animated recent European intellectual debate, reading Herbert Spencer, Charles Darwin, H T Buckle, Carl Voigt and John Stuart Mill. She also changed her name from 'Emilie' to 'Olive'.

In the wake of an unhappy episode when she believed herself to be engaged to an older Swiss man, Julius Gau, she rejoined Theo and Ettie in 1872 at the tent city which had grown up around New Rush, the richest of the diamond diggings. It was to this very unsettled period of her life that she dated the onset of the respiratory pains and asthma that were to dog her for the rest of her life – a condition probably not helped by her later fondness for cigarettes. At Kimberley, as New Rush was renamed in the following year, she taught in the evening school, began to write her first short stories and nursed the dream of an education abroad, possibly as a doctor, should Theo strike lucky.

In 1874, the family finances being no better, she embarked upon a series of governessing posts, which, in remoter homes, often encompassed the work of a general family factotum, helping out in a shop, correcting proofs for a newspaper-owning employer or mending the family's clothes: one employer paid her less because she felt unable to teach his children religion. Meanwhile she continued to write, working on drafts of three novels, *Undine, From Man to Man* and *The Story of an African Farm*, and saved whatever she could to achieve her independence. By 1881 her father was dead, her mother had found a home in a convent, and Schreiner felt free to sail for England to begin the nurse's training offered free to single women.

She saw England as an alternative home: an elder brother, Fred, or 'dadda' as Schreiner called him, was running a school in Eastbourne, and Will was studying law at Cambridge. The several fresh starts she made upon a medical training each came to nothing when her health repeatedly failed her. Diagnoses of Schreiner's chronic illness have usually favoured a psychosomatic explanation, relating its origin to suppression or denial of her sexual identity, but the incidence of her attacks makes it equally possible to interpret them as offering a form of safeguard for life as a writer. Understandably depressed at still being supported, this time by Fred, and lonely in her London lodgings, she resorted to frequent self-medication with patent medicines. These remedies, which often contained laudanum, together with the strychnine recommended by doctors and the potassium bromide that she believed to be useful in curbing sexual urges, must have formed a powerful and unpredictable medical cocktail, contributing to the bouts of sleeplessness and the lurid dreams and nightmares that fuelled some of the pieces reprinted in this book.

Meanwhile, the manuscript of *The Story of an African Farm* was doing the rounds of the publishers and was finally accepted in January 1883 by George Meredith, reader for the firm of Chapman and Hall and a freethinker who was to prove sympathetic to the challenge to the dominant sexual ideology posed by 'new woman' fiction. This largely autobiographically-based novel, whose heroine, Lyndall, despite her advanced views on gender relations, suffers the fate of many another fictional 'fallen sister' of the Victorian period, proved a *succès de scandale*, being recognised by several leading reviewers as introducing a new tone to the moral, religious and sexual debate: it was consequently banned by some libraries. Although published under the pseudonym 'Ralph Iron', the secret of the novel's authorship quickly circulated literary London. Three editions appeared in the first year and a further twelve in Schreiner's lifetime.

The novel's earnest exposition of the two main characters' adolescent struggles to make out for themselves a philosophy and a way of life to challenge the harsh fundamentalist religion of a society in which young women were seen as little more than pawns in the larger game of marriage and property, struck a chord with a range of young avant-garde intellectuals in England who saw themselves as engaged in similar ideological crusades. Over the next three years, Eleanor Marx, Havelock Ellis, Edward Carpenter and Karl Pearson became friends, introducing her to debating circles such as the Progressive Association, the Fellowship of the New Life, and the Men and Women's Club, but Schreiner never unreservedly affiliated herself with any of these collectivist or individualist experiments in socialism. The synthesis she pursued between her passionate sense of individuality and her universalist convictions was too spiritual in aspiration and expression to find a final resting-place in the scientific materialism colouring much of the progressive social, sexual and political debate of the 1880s (see Rive 101–2). She also seems to have found the probing mutual exploration made possible by intimate friendship more conducive to articulating her own position than the cut and thrust of group debate which, even when discussing the injustice of contemporary gender relations, often tended to be dominated by male voices and attitudes (Walkowitz).

In *Woman and Labour* (1911), a book that grew out of her argument with Karl Pearson, Professor of Mathematics at University College, London, and subsequent eugenicist, Olive was to opine that the 'sex relationships may assume almost any form on earth as the conditions of life vary' (12). Attempting to live out the life of her ideas, however, brought difficulties: visits from unaccompanied men led to rows with landladies, and her enthusiasm for befriending prostitutes did nothing to improve her reputation as a respectable lodger.

Schreiner formed a series of close relationships with the founders of the new psychology of sex. The first, with the young medical student, Havelock Ellis, survived a brief, unsuccessful attempt at sexual intimacy and continued in a friendship which was to survive both their unconventional marriages. Transferring her attentions to Karl Pearson, she reminded him: 'The great danger which we who would fight for or lead humanity have to guard against is the mixing up of our personal interest with the things we fight for. Keep thy hands pure and thy head pure and thy heart pure from any touch of self" (Rive 112). Bound by the terms of a friendship founded on intellectual equality, that she had herself negotiated, she strenuously denied that any element of 'sex love' had arisen on her side, though admitting that she would have 'struck ... dead' any woman who had succeeded in seducing this ascetic idealist (Draznin 427). Meanwhile, she felt guilty at having unwittingly won the love of another of this set, her physician, Brian Donkin.

Increasingly dependent on Donkin's morphine injections and prescriptions from Ellis, she retreated to two Catholic convents before leaving England in December 1886 to restore her shattered health and self-possession. Until October 1889, Schreiner moved restlessly, and usually alone, between Switzerland, France and Italy, occasionally making forays to England to visit Carpenter and his, predominantly, homosocial, circle of socialist friends. As was her custom, she continued to work on several projects simultaneously: an unfinished novel (*From Man to Man*), a never-completed introduction to Mary Wollstonecraft's *Vindication of the Rights of Woman*, the work of another troubled proto-feminist, and more of the allegorical dreams which had always formed part of her writer's palette. Allegory appealed to her as a form, she told the publisher Ernest Rhys, because in it 'I can condense five or six pages into one, with no loss, but a great gain to clearness' (Rive 136).

When she returned to London in the summer of 1889, ready to sail for South Africa that autumn, she took lodgings in the East End, far from her former associates. There she saw something of the Great Dock strike, and formed a friendship with Amy Levy, the Jewish poet-novelist, cut short by Levy's suicide. Before leaving England, Schreiner unsuccessfully 'spent all the last days waiting in the rain', outside University College, for a glimpse of Pearson (Rive 146).

Once back in South Africa, Schreiner found the people 'three hundred years behind the times' (Rive 162) and the climate an irritant to her asthma, so that she was soon forced to establish her base in Matjesfontein, an inland health resort accessible from Cape Town and near to the Great Karoo plateau landscape which she had loved since childhood. The Schreiner family were now a force to be reckoned with in

*Introduction* xiii

South Africa. Ettie and Theo were noted for their temperance work and for their support of the coloured, the natives and the destitute. Will, currently legal adviser to the Governor of the Cape, would twice serve as Attorney-General, and become Prime Minister for the Cape Colony (1898–1900); and the success of *The Story of an African Farm* had turned Schreiner herself into a Cape celebrity. As if to mark this watershed in her life, she sent the manuscript of *Dreams*, a collection including writing done in both South Africa and Europe, to Havelock Ellis to launch in Britain, although the preface gives her address as Matjesfontein and the dedicatee was her niece, Ursula, a third-generation colonial. The three stories comprising *Dream Life and Real Life* (1893) and 'The Buddhist Priest's Wife' also date from this period. Although she thought this last tale of unrequited love her best work to date, she probably suppressed it as 'too personal' (Rive 208). In a final letter to Pearson, who had married in 1890, Schreiner told him that his steely focus had taught her the 'gross immorality' of indiscriminate sympathy: the unspoken lesson he had offered had been 'the man or woman who will spend his life for his fellows must look calmly, wisely over life and say here and here I can best spend myself' (Rive 179). She now turned increasingly to analyses of the colony's political, social and natural life.

Her initial admiration for the forceful personality of Cecil Rhodes waned as she recognised how the commercial interests of British imperialism, which he personified, were inevitably bent upon dominating or eradicating any opposition to the vision of an industrially-successful colony. Her first, unpublished, critique, 'The salvation of a Ministry' (Cronwright-Schreiner 202–5) was a political satire, cast in the form of a dream, which plays out topical events on the wider stage before God's Judgment seat: it also demonstrated Schreiner's habit of eliding the cause of women with that of other racially, politically and economically oppressed groups.

In the 1890s it seemed to Schreiner that the Boers (or Afrikaners), rural settlers of predominantly Dutch and German descent, whose language and shared Calvinist faith held them together, were becoming at first the dupes and then the victims of Rhodes' expansionist ambitions. In a series of essays, posthumously collected as *Thoughts on South Africa* (1923), she sought to explain Boer culture to an English-speaking readership. While she often found it intellectually suffocating during her governessing period, she also saw, in the simple life of Boer farmsteads, values that might provide an alternative to the dehumanising forces of capitalism. Her anti-Rhodes stance did nothing to improve her relations with those in her family who valued their British heritage.

Meanwhile, however, she had found the possibility of alternative support in Samuel Cronwright, a freethinking admirer, eight years her junior. In mid 1893 she retreated to England for six months to contemplate the changes entailed were she, at 38, to marry a farmer anxious for children – even one prepared to treat her as a genius and change his name to Cronwright-Schreiner. In opting for him, she thought, she would be discarding her old ideal of 'the man of thought and fine-drawn feelings like ... Ellis and Karl Pearson', realising a mutual sexual attraction, and 'becoming a sort of small Napoleon' by marrying the kind of man who needed her for his 'moral education' (Rive 223). Despite her insistence upon the 'new woman's' economic rights and duties, Schreiner's thinking was still much imbued with the notion of Victorian woman's redemptive mission. They were married in a civil ceremony on 24 February 1894. Life as a farmer's wife was to be short-lived: her recurrent asthma attacks persuaded 'Cron' to abandon farming and accompany her to Kimberley where, in two years, she reckoned, she could earn the £30,000 necessary to make them independent (Cronwright-Schreiner 271). It was here that she gave birth, on

30 April 1895, to an apparently healthy daughter who survived for only sixteen hours; there were to be three miscarriages in the following year.

She and Cron found another outlet for mutual endeavour in jointly denouncing Rhodes' opportunism. The disastrous Jameson Raid of 1895, in which Rhodes, ostensibly acting to defend the interests of non-Afrikaner Europeans, had planned to annex the Boer Republic of the Tansvaal in order to exploit its recently discovered gold, proved Schreiner's worst fears. Rhodes' next enterprise of 'pacifying' the Mashona and the Matabele, who stood in the way of British expansion northward, stung her into writing a further allegorical indictment of his policies: *Trooper Peter Halket of Mashonaland* (1897). This tale of an English working-class boy's awakening to the rape of South Africa which he and his like were perpetrating was aimed at a British readership, intoxicated by tales of colonial derring-do and the Empire's civilising mission (Burdett 124–35). Travelling to England to arrange for the book's publication, the Cronwright-Scheiners found themselves fellow-passengers with Rhodes, on his way to defend his conduct in the Jameson Raid. In London one or two Church leaders responded to Schreiner's message, but a public fired by the imperial self-congratulation of Queen Victoria's Jubilee year was not receptive.

Despite Schreiner's ill-health, she and Cron managed a European tour, before returning to South Africa that autumn. It had now become clear to Cron that, however carefully he nursed her, she seemed incapable of completing larger, income-generating works: *An English South African's View of the Situation* (1899) only made it into print by dint of Cron and his brother acting as copy-editors. Cron had, meanwhile, decided to article himself to a lawyer in Johannesburg. His increasingly public stance on political matters took him as an anti-war campaigner to Britain soon after the outbreak of the Boer War, where he was described in Parliament as 'an Englishman who married a German lady' (First and Scott 238). Meanwhile, despite her antipathy to public speaking, Schreiner was making passionate contributions to women's anti-war congresses in South Africa. On Cron's return they moved, under the isolating circumstances of martial law, to Hanover, an Afrikaner township, where she wrote 'Eighteen-ninety-nine'. When the war ended Cron was able to find legal work and was soon elected to the Cape Parliament, but Schreiner felt no less beleaguered: the Afrikaners began 'to remember that I am English and don't go to church, and a "Liberal" in religious matters, and it makes life very lonely' (First and Scott 251). The move, in 1907, to a house Cron had built in De Aar, a small township on a railway line, brought the couple no closer: her chronic restlessness and habit of pacing the house by night scarcely accorded with her husband's working routines.

Instead she joined her brother Will, now a defender of the native African interest, in debating South Africa's post-war constitution. Her affinity with the purposes of the South African Woman's Enfranchisement League foundered over its internal division as to whether to wage the campaign for enfranchisement on behalf of white women only. In 1911 she published *Woman and Labour*, a fragment recalled from a lengthier, unrevised manuscript, burnt, she claimed, in the sacking of her Johannesburg house by British troops in 1899. This book had its origins in the sex-debates of the 1880s, but its completion under the conditions of martial law gave its thoughts about women's position in relation to the modern market-place, and their gendered perceptions of war, a contemporary currency that was to make it a formative text for female pacifists in World War I.

With the tide of events in South Africa now flowing strongly against her, Schreiner took ship for Europe again in 1913. The solicitude of London friends and admirers was, however, insufficient to improve her health or lift her spirits and she soon sought cures on the continent, where she found herself when war broke in August 1914. She was not to see Cron again until 1920, though they corresponded by every mail. Returning to England, she found that her alien surname made difficulties. Furthermore, the war served to polarise adherents of those causes to which she was chiefly devoted. Her anti-racist enthusiasm for Ghandi's non-violent struggle in India came to an abrupt halt when she discovered his endorsement of the British stance in this war, and her South African hackles were raised by the imperial convictions she detected at the heart of the female pacifist movement in Britain. Her relations with brother Will were also tested when, as South Africa's ambassador to London, he lent support to the British campaign. She put her name to the anti-conscription cause and to the demand for equal pay for women workers. Two anti-war pieces, 'Who Knocks at the Door', and the posthumously published 'The Dawn of Civilisation', also date from this period.

When Cron arrived in London in July 1920, having sold up in South Africa, he found his wife 'aged greatly' (Cronwright-Schreiner 374). They were to have only a month together, because Schreiner, believing that Cron planned an extended trip to America, had already booked her return sailing, preferring, as she said, to 'end my life in my own country and among my own people' (First and Scott 321). Back in South Africa, suffering as always from poor health, she resumed a solitary boarding-house life in Cape Town where she died on 10 December 1920. There were no religious observances at her funeral. A year later, Cron reunited her remains with that of her baby, and a much-loved dog, on a kop, looking out over the Karoo, that she had identified in the early months of their marriage. Also in accordance with her wishes, Cron set up a woman's medical scholarship to be awarded without reference to race, colour or religion.

I have given a detailed account of the circumstances of Schreiner's life not because I want to suggest that her work should simply be seen as an artistically naïve, transparent window on her life, but because the cultural conditions in which this work was produced are important to an understanding of its artistry. The move, initiated in her husband's biography in 1924, to present Olive Schreiner as wholly exceptional: 'a woman of genius, so strange and incredible in her personality ... it seemed to me there was no standard of comparison between her and normal or even abnormal persons' has been damaging in a number of ways (Cronwright-Schreiner vii–viii). Deprived of a context, her thought and writing can be variously manipulated into being viewed as eccentric, and therefore, by implication, marginal to the central intellectual debates of the era; the product of an untutored genius, that is, the work of an empty vessel filled by greater forces, implicitly or explicitly defined as male; or, so peculiar as to put them, or the parts that critics wish to denigrate, beyond the reaches of rational analysis. This last and simplest manoeuvre is readily illustrated in the introduction to Susan R. Horton's *Difficult Women, Artful Lives*: 'The flip side of the stolid, sensible, diligent political activist was, perhaps inevitably, the frustrated headbanger she quite literally was' (xiii). It is the first two ways of demeaning her work, marginality and naïveté, that I now want to address.

'All Europe had contributed to the making of Kurtz', Joseph Conrad tells us in his anti-imperialist tale, *Heart of Darkness* (1902). As a child of mixed European origin, Schreiner enjoyed a similarly complex inheritance, growing up in a colony where Europe, and more specifically Britain, was still thought of as the cultural centre to which boys at least were sent 'home' for education. Conversely their distance from 'the centre' rendered the colonists automatically culturally inferior in the eyes of their British counterparts. The timbre of this cultural contempt comes across very clearly in Virginia Woolf's 1925 review of Cron's edition of *The Letters of Olive Schreiner*: her first paragraph complains of the unsifted 'jumble and muddle of odds and ends ... all of which are related as if Olive Schreiner were a figure of the highest importance', instead of 'rather distant and unfamiliar'. She acknowledges Schreiner's contribution to the cause of emancipation of women and concedes a brilliance and power, that 'reminds us inevitably of the Brontë novels', to *The Story of an African Farm*, but continues, 'it has the limitations of those egotistical masterpieces without a full measure of their strength. The writer's interests are local, her passions personal ...' (Woolf, *Essays*, 4–6).

By 'local' Woolf implies that the colonial setting automatically limits Schreiner's capacity 'to enter with sympathy into the experiences of minds differing from her own': the mind in question, of course, is one nurtured in the upper-class environs of Bloomsbury, accustomed to writing for 'the daughters of educated men' (Woolf, *Guineas*, passim), and to patronising the 'self-made' writers of her acquaintance. Among English modernist writers only D. H. Lawrence seems to have felt Schreiner's influence: having been lent a copy of *The Story of an African Farm* by Helen Corke, he recommended it to Jessie Chambers and borrowed the device of 'The Stranger' for an early version of *The Trespasser* (Worthen 258–9). But then Lawrence, like Schreiner, was of provincial, Dissenting, working-class origins and it was for this audience, and particularly its women constituents, who felt that the South African heroine's plight articulated something of their own, that Schreiner's novel then held its most widely-attested appeal (First and Scott 121).

As a political activist Schreiner was strongly aware of the need to tailor material to a specific audience or audiences, a consciousness that was all the more important when a plurality of market-places was opening up, as 'high-brow' coterie literature sought to distance itself from 'low-brow' popular literature. In practice Schreiner's habit of targeting different readerships probably also had its effect in diluting her reputation. Only five years after her death she had already become, for Virginia Woolf, the author of 'one remarkable novel and a few other fragmentary works which no admirer of *The Story of an African Farm* would care to place beside it' (Woolf, *Essays*, 4), while for those who followed affairs in South Africa she was just as likely to be known for her pro-Boer interventions, or her anti-(Boer)-War campaigning. The only writings that she placed first in South Africa, rather than with London publishers, were the essays and newspaper articles designed to have an impact on political attitudes within the colony: the main body of her writing – whether concerned with European attitudes to South Africa, issues of gender or race, or her fiction – was offered first to London publishers. Schreiner was a knowing beneficiary of the nineteenth century's process of literary democratisation, claiming that 'the press has taken the place of the ruler ... Even more clearly the novel has taken the place of other forms of art in carrying to the heart of the people the truths (or untruths) of the Age' (Rive 109). Her awareness of these trends in the market-place made her very specific about the mode of production's ability to create particular audiences: in 1892 she wrote to T. Fisher Unwin, who was to publish each of the three volumes incorporated in the present volume,

> I insisted on African Farm being published at 1/- because the book was published by me for working men. I wanted to feel sure boys like Waldo, could buy a copy, and feel they were not alone. I have again, last year, at the request of my publisher, allowed it to be printed at 3/6 as I felt sure most poor lads would have it within reach ... Dreams is not published by me with the special intention of reaching the poor. I

would prefer the rich to have it. If I dedicated it to the public, I should dedicate it 'To all Capitalists, Millionaires and Middlemen in England and America and all high and mighty persons.' It is a book which will always have its own public of cultured persons who will have it at any price. It will probably be a far more valuable property in 15 or 20 years than it is at present, as the younger generation grows up and the older dies out. I feel this with regard to all my books; therefore except for a very large sum, I will never sell the copyright nor any right except that of printing them during my pleasure. (Rive 209)

These dreams, stories and allegories, which have been, for the most part, lost to view for the better part of a century, were not seen as 'occasional' in the same sense as her more overtly political writings, nor as an attempt to find a voice which might prove accessible to the least educated. Her reference to a 'public of cultured persons who will have it at any price' suggests that she saw these tales as bearing the weight of whatever literary reputation she was to acquire. By presenting the two volumes she published in her own lifetime as artefacts that might stand fair to become collectors' items she also hoped to attract the rich and powerful readers who, once awakened, would be in the best position to put her vision into effect. The first edition of *Dreams*, which retailed at six shillings, sold out in four days (Rive 184); the surrealistic cover bore a stylised, embossed, copper-coloured sun setting over a blue ocean on which rests a sun-dial bearing the name of Olive Schreiner round its rim. By the eighth edition a new Art Nouveau cover had been designed in red, yellow, black and green, depicting buttercups growing near the margins of a pool, reaching upwards until they come to rest against a red brick wall on the front cover, and approach the title line on the spine. Inside, the volume bears the publisher's pseudo-classical bookplate, and each separate tale is begun with a small, individual frieze of intricately woven flowers and mythical figures. The opening capital letter of each tale is decorated in the manner of an illuminated manuscript and at the conclusion of most tales is another, individually-drawn, floral motif. *Dream Life and Real Life*, a slim volume in T. Fisher Unwin's 'Pseudonym Library', is a work of more restrained elegance – the cloth cover bearing black lines and the publisher's stamp as decoration – but the three tales similarly begin with a frieze and illuminated capital. The posthumous *Stories, Dreams and Allegories,* published in the economic austerity of post-War Britain, is an altogether more workaday affair. During her lifetime, however, both Chapman and Hall and T. Fisher Unwin regarded her work sufficiently highly to bow to her wishes in matters of both content and appearance.

The care with which Schreiner placed her work in the literary market-place offers a partial rebuttal of the critical tradition that would cast her as a naïve artist, subject to the promptings of involuntary impulse, rather than exerting artistic command over her material. The simple vocabulary and sentence structure, the stylised speech patterns and the overtly Biblical rhythms that Schreiner employed in the dreams and allegories could be taken for the artlessness of a writer accustomed to writing for children. The formulaic questions and answers, by which visions are unfolded and meanings sought, certainly emulate the catechistic exchanges beloved in Victorian schoolbooks, though the habitual naïveté with which interlocutors ask for alternative explanations of the scenes of cruelty and oppression, accepted as normal by the participants, also contains its own disconcerting critique of a world where lies and half-truths form the common currency. Her style was in any case sufficiently distinctive to invite contemporary parodies (Rive 186). It is, however, not difficult to see how her own occasional accounts of her creative process contributed to a notion of Schreiner as an inspired hysteric. In 1889 Arthur Symons, overcome by the eight-hour audience 'the great woman' had granted him ('The George Sands, George Eliots pale before her incredible ardency', he gushed), attempted to reconstruct the flow of her self-revelation (Cronwright-Schreiner 184–90).

> This is very characteristic. Once in Paris she was writing an allegory – I think the 'Three Dreams in a Desert' – and she had done only a part. She was walking over one of the bridges across the Seine, when suddenly all flashed upon her. She screamed aloud, and began to run up the Boulevard St. Michel, and ran till she came to her lodgings, when she sat down and never rose till the allegory was finished. Was this the time when she wrote for twenty-four hours without tasting food?

Beside this recollection, Cron added the corrective note, 'The allegory in question was "The Sunlight Lay Across My Bed"', a tale over which, she told Symons, she had 'agonized' for three months. The reworking and rewriting which made her work so notoriously difficult to complete were out of kilter with the sybilline presence Symons wanted to meet. Schreiner's frequently-remarked magnetic personality must have made her appear suitable for refashioning to the cabalistic interests of the world in which Symons was already mixing and from which he would produce *The Symbolist Movement in Literature* (1899), celebrating the reverie and symbols employed by contemporary French writers to evoke the subtle relations between the spiritual and the material world.

> It ('The Sunlight Lay Across My Bed') is music, and a picture; I saw the picture as, in her wonderful low voice, she told me of it, and recited parts, her voice sometimes dying down almost to an inaudible whisper. Of the banquet, and the red wine, and how the horror grows on you, and you find out that the wine is blood: and then the winepress in the background: 'And one said, it is the crying of the grapes. And God said, I hear'. (Her voice chanting softly as she spoke.) The whole of it she hears as if set to music, and she despairs of making other people hear it just so – as in this – and in the crescendo of the Church Service. And it ends with her waking up in her room (the room at Gore Street) and hearing the strains of the barrel organ ('Everybody laughs at it – but you won't laugh') with its sense of the impotent striving after the perfect and the beautiful. This allegory has all her Socialistic strivings, and thus, at present, all her soul.

Writing from Paris two months earlier, however, Schreiner had been concerned to avoid the 'awful temptation ... of delicious sensation' into which the blank verse rhythms of this particular dream had been 'unconsciously' falling: 'I find I've been writing sort of verse that scans the whole time ... Damned if I shan't write plain prose now right on to the end and get the thing done' (Rive 155).

Symons' involvement in the exoticism of contemporary mystical movements perhaps masked for him the echoes of the more obvious common religious heritage he shared with Schreiner: both their fathers had been Methodist ministers. Schreiner's fondness for the dream form and the allegory – it is not clear to what extent she distinguished between the two – has been variously attributed to a Romantic strain acquired from Gottlob, to the influence of Dante, and of Bunyan's *Pilgrim's Progress*, the last, at least, forming staple reading in most nineteenth-century Protestant households. However, the imagery of wine-presses, and of communal feasting upon the

*Introduction* xix

wine formed from the blood of suffering, points to the Bible as their common source. Almost throughout both the Old and New Testaments, dreams, visions and parables anticipate explanations, which, when they occur, are often almost as mystifying as the stories they seek to illuminate. It was to her 'own language of parables' that she felt forced to resort in 1892 when explaining her religious position to a clergyman experiencing difficulties with his faith. 'If I must put it into words', she conceded, 'I would say; the Universe is one, and, it lives: or if you would put it into older phraseology, I would say: *There is NOTHING but God*'. Christianity had lost its appeal for her because, rejecting her sense of God's immanence in a universe where birth and death could both be incorporated in 'endless existence', it insisted on confining incarnation to the person of Christ, and so fostered a 'scorn for the animal world, and the hatred of matter' (Rive 212–14). Her spiritual beliefs, which seem to have changed very little from her teenage years to her last testament in 'The Dawn of Civilisation', owed much to the writings of Ralph Waldo Emerson, from whose name she probably took both the names of characters in *The Story of an African Farm*, and her pseudonym, 'Ralph Iron' (Showalter, *Literature* 199; Gilbert and Gubar 241). Like many Victorian freethinkers, Emerson and Schreiner felt free to rifle the terminology of orthodox faith, reinterpreting such words as 'soul', 'immortality', or 'God' to incorporate elements of other philosophies that attracted them. Emerson's belief in a unifying Over-Soul permeating the universe held an obvious appeal to those originally nurtured by Protestantism because it permitted significance to the individual being as a microcosm latently containing the meaning of the whole. This way of relating the whole to the parts also seemed, in Schreiner's eclectic philosophy, to map neatly onto Herbert Spencer's belief in a unity underlying nature. An Emersonian approach could also be deployed to offset the more depressing aspects of an evolutionary theory which, in insisting upon immutable, universal patterns, minimised the importance of the individual moral struggle.

Schreiner's own birthright had been an idealistic missionary vision, born out of discontent with the world as it actually was, and a consequent belief in the possibility of change. Removing the compensatory promise of an otherworldly afterlife only made the task more urgent, and the disappointments encountered in terrestrial life more dispiriting. The undoubted pathos of a tale such as 'Three Dreams in a Desert' derives from the way in which the allegorical figure of 'Woman', first discovered by the dreamer's gaze as a supine object, bound, in the course of the social evolutionary process, by the 'Inevitable Necessity' of 'the Age-of-dominion-of-muscular-force', attains individual subjectivity. The 'creature's' struggles form the object lesson of scientific inquiry, but, as she achieves the physical and mental resilience to make her way to the river barring the way to the Land of Freedom, she is given a voice only to proclaim the Modernist predicament: '*Oh, I am alone! I am utterly alone!*' She is persuaded by old man 'Reason' to become part of the bridge over which 'the entire human race' will eventually pass, at which point the dream breaks again: the concluding dream reverts to a generic vision of future bliss in which women and men walk hand in hand and the androgynous dreamer's voice offers the undifferentiated community of an ant colony and the certainty that the sun will rise on the morrow as nature's corroboration of evolutionary meliorism. The fractured nature of this dream sequence, together with the changing vantage-points from which the tale is told, suggest a series of unresolved tensions: Protestant conviction in the importance of the individual moral stance has encountered the totalising scientific narratives of Darwinian and eugenic thought; and the individual female voice, offering an emotional response to a particular predicament, emerges only for abstract reason to

xx    *Introduction*

reconsign it to the position of undifferentiated object of an androgynous gaze. The effect was, in part at least, deliberate. 'Three Dreams in a Desert' had been written, as part of the earlier version of the 'sex-book' (Schreiner 16), designed to counter Pearson's approach in his opening paper for the Men and Women's Club, which, she complained, had been 'entirely wrong' in laying out 'woman, her needs, her mental and physical nature' as a scientific object for man to analyse (First and Scott 148). The form she had therefore chosen for her own 'sex-book' mingled two genres so as to restore the balance disturbed by Pearson, that 'sworn enemy of the emotions' (Rive 94).

> In addition to the prose argument I had in each chapter one or more allegories; because while it is easy clearly to express abstract thoughts in argumentative prose, whatever emotion those thoughts awaken I have not felt myself able adequately to express. (Schreiner 16)

This declaration of aesthetic intent has frequently been invoked by critics eager to locate Schreiner's use of non-realist genres within a specifically female tradition. Such readings encourage us to interpret women writers' investment in dream, vision and allegory as a gendered admission of women's powerlessness to intervene in the particular historical moment. The prophetic voice and the appeal to an imagined future, runs this argument, allow women to envisage and hope for solutions for which immediate social or political circumstances offer no authority. It would be hard to deny that some of Schreiner's fables, such as 'Seeds A-Growing', which offers a ringing affirmation that every political injustice sows the harvest of the spirit of freedom, seem naïve in the light of terrorist organisations' frequent claims that each such act breeds new converts to violence. Non-realist genres can be variously interpreted as, at worst, escapist substitutes for political engagement and, at best, models for future empowerment, offering a critical vantage-point external to the narratives of patriarchy. Schreiner's dreams and allegories have been subjected to both extremes of this theoretical approach, since the move they make to escape the dualism of real and ideal, can also be interpreted as a re-inscription of that very binary divide.

Her longest socialist fable, 'The Sunlight Lay Across My Bed', attempts to address this problem by bringing the dreamer back from his visions of Hell and Heaven to 'dull grey' London streetlife and the noise of the 'broken barrel-organ' penetrating dingy bed-sit land. The responsibility for bringing these alternative global visions to bear upon quotidian reality lies, the ending makes clear, in individual commitment to realising the ideal. The title of her last piece, 'The Dawn of Civilisation', draws deliberate attention to this problem of form. Subtitling it with such phrases as 'stray thoughts' or 'homely personal confession' she contextualises it as 'woman's writing', personal, intimate, and unwilling to pretend to logical coherence, and then immediately proceeds to an impersonally argued analysis of the various ways in which a man might come to be a conscientious objector. The second part resorts to the confessional, the visionary and the prophetic. However, perhaps because the central experience she recounts was pre-pubertal, her account of a personally transforming vision is not inflected by gender concerns. The very frequency with which Schreiner employs an androgynous or a male voice for her dreamers suggests that she was anxious to ward off the danger of her visions being read as specifically female. In 'In A Ruined Chapel' she presents 'sex' as one of the accidental 'outward attributes of time, place and circumstance' that threaten to politicise affairs properly belonging to the whole 'soul' of mankind, while in 'The Sunlight Lay Across My Bed', God tells the dreamer, 'In the least heaven sex reigns supreme; in the higher it is not noticed; but in the highest it does not exist'.

The obvious appeal of a gender-related theory of genre, for dealing with an artist herself so interested in 'the woman question', should also be tempered by recollecting the range of male writers at the end of the nineteenth and beginning of the twentieth centuries who employed symbol, dream, vision and allegory. William Butler Yeats' later visionary systems and their mystical overtone would have been abhorrent to Schreiner, but could equally be seen as a mode for accommodating both personal failure and a pessimistic assessment of contemporary society, as mere 'phases' within far longer cycles that would prove capable of redressing all temporary setbacks.

Her interest in the exploration of the function and nature of the unconscious was also a non-gender-specific characteristic of the period. She shared with Havelock Ellis a view of the unconscious as linked to physiological process, but her ability to see it also as the originating seat of the symbolic, aligned her with the new psychoanalytic interest in the collective unconscious (Berkman 200–202). Such theories were particularly useful to the many competing voices who wished to lay a claim to universality for idealist beliefs which had been hammered out on the anvil of personal experience. Finding an imaginative expression, accessible to a wider readership, for highly individualistic, quasi-religious philosophies achieved wide currency in an age marked by the apparent breakdown of orthodox religious, moral and social consensus. In this respect the high seriousness with which 'The Artist's Secret' treats the artist's vocation links Schreiner's aesthetic to a Modernist sensibility.

Her use of dream visions as a form for criticising patriarchy, Empire and capitalism can also be identified as belonging to a far wider literary turn. Ursula Brangwen's vision of the rainbow, which would be rooted in the blood of the 'sordid people who crept hard-scaled and separate' to build a new world (Lawrence 496; ch. 15), bears clear analogies to 'the bridge which shall be built with our bodies' seen by the woman in 'Three Dreams in a Desert'. The notion of genre as itself offering a protest from the margins against the tropes favoured by the centre, found favour with three other contemporaries entitled to claim 'colonial' status: Wilde, Yeats and Joyce. Yeats published *Fairy and Folk Tales of the Irish Peasantry*, voicing the stories of the poor, colonised and disreputable, in the same year, 1887, that Wilde's allegorical fairy-tale, 'The Happy Prince', laid bare the unheeding proximity of the extremes of wealth and poverty. Wilde described his tale as 'an attempt to treat a high and modern problem in a form that aims at delicacy and imaginative treatment: it is a reaction against the purely imitative character of modern art (Wilde 355}. However much James Joyce strove to assert the European, Dante Alighieri, as his model, he might also be seen as most entering into his inheritance as a British colonial subject when he recognised the advantages of symbol, prophecy and vision for freeing Stephen Dedalus from the 'nets' of 'nationality, language, religion' (Joyce 203).

Allegory, as ethnographic critics such as James Clifford and Laura Donaldson have pointed out, was a useful device for writers engaged in contemplating the different cultures thrown together in the process of empire-building (Clifford 140–62; Donaldson 134). The Conrad of *Heart of Darkness* and the Schreiner of 'Who Knocks at the Door', or 'Dream Life and Real Life: A Little African Story' are involved in acts of translation which attempt both to establish a metanarrative allowing readers rooted in one culture to glimpse the *mores* of another, and, at the same time, to destabilise assumptions that see meaning and moral value as an inherent possession of the centre and thus to be mediated by the dominating race to those existing at the outposts of civilisation. The temporal dislocation of dream in 'Who Knocks at the Door' allows Schreiner to establish the common human inheritance and the iterativeness of the historical process that Conrad's opening recollections of the Roman invasion of Britain effect in his tale. In 'A Little African Story' the details of landscape are used to disconcerting effect in a tale that drifts in and out of dream-consciousness. Just at the point when the exotic or unknown 'prickly pear' and 'kippersol', found by Jannita in the wilderness, identify this as a tale alien to English readers' experience, the narrator calls them back into connection by familiarising the flora: 'she went out and picked some of those purple little ground flowers – you know them – those that keep their faces close to the ground'. The coalition of greed, formed by an *English* navvy, a Hottentot and a Bushman, that threatens the Boer homestead, and murders the orphan-child standing in its way, is thus brought home to the reader as at once a localised tale and a wider allegory of the opportunistic alliances of empire.

By imposing arbitrary meaning, allegory can resist the apparent 'natural' relationship and values, often cemented by literary tradition, between symbol and symbolised, and render transparent the 'appropriation' and 'essentialising' that often accompany the process of characterisation in realist fiction. Although 'little Jannita', in this story, is, unusually for Schreiner's 'dream' works, given a name, she has no history or particularising characteristics of which we can be certain: we are never deceived into seeing her as more than a 'type' of child-victim, fashioned by Schreiner for the exclusive purposes of this tale. The narrator's voice positions Jannita as object of a moralised commentary, and her voice, when it is briefly heard, offers no illusion of subjectivity. If we are tempted to see Jannita's 'home-making' instincts up among the 'kopjes', or her desire to save even her oppressors, as indicative of a universal feminine instinct, the story firmly resists this by describing the farmer's wife and daughter whom she has saved, retreating to the kitchen, making a great fire and 'singing psalms all the while', thus drowning out the voice of the child beyond their walls: Jannita may be a white girl, but she is also a mere wage-slave, equally expendable in the cause of marauding freebooters or Boer economy. This small girl's freedom consists of her power to exile herself, her ability to dream of another, better, existence and her capacity for moral choice, none of which save her from an early burial in a nameless mound.

For later generations of feminist readers brought up to revel in tales of feisty, self-determining heroines, Schreiner's stories have a dispiriting habit of weighing all too carefully the costs of idealism. Her allegorical women feel to the full the physical pain and emotional desolation of the renunciations they are called upon to make in pursuit of a future, only to be dreamt of, in which men and women will enjoy the mutuality of equal companionship. 'In a Far-Off World' rehearses, in schematic mode, a message Schreiner was fond of reworking. The price of giving 'the best of all gifts' to the loved one is paid for with the heart's blood, and results in the freedom of the beloved to depart without explanation. The woman's self-sacrificial role is strongly reminiscent of the mid-Victorian understanding of woman's place in the theology of atonement, that Schreiner would have been taught as a child, and the accompanying trope of self-mutilation owes much to the Christian imagery of the self-wounding pelican mother, so beloved of Renaissance painters of the crucifixion. The secularised eschatology of this tale indeed seems to insist upon a religious framework: the woman's 'prayer' is successful because she makes it upon 'the steps of the stone altar' in the

*Introduction* xxiii

forest shrine, and her inner desire is interrogated by a disembodied voice with the power to answer prayer. Here the voice is genderless, but, disconcertingly for readers accustomed to the liberating gender-play often found in late twentieth century reworkings of myth, Schreiner's tales all too frequently position a suffering, akin to masochism, as female and allow it to be inflicted by male figures, appearing variously as 'Duty' or 'Love'.

Nevertheless, the punitive aspects of the theology of her childhood were counterbalanced by the certain promise of a better future held out by the same religious vision. In her allegories and dreams, solitary pain and suffering are often validated by the unquestioned authority of an external, non-terrestrial, voice to whom the future is already known. Where this external authority is absent from her moral fables, as in 'The Wax Doll and the Stepmother' and 'The Adventures of Master Towser', two tales she wrote for children during her time as a governess, sentimentality is inclined to take over. For later readers, acutely aware of the crushing disappointments suffered by New Women, and less attuned to the faith in the evolutionary imperative, this bargain between present pain and deferred joy seems either meretricious or unintelligible. Elaine Showalter, for instance, reads 'Life's Gifts' as expressive of 'the bitterness and disillusionment of New Women with men who were not ready to join them in their evolutionary progress' (*Anarchy* 56–7). The deserted woman's assertion of contentment at the close of 'In a Far-Off World' is paralleled in 'Life's Gifts' by a woman laughing in her sleep when Life promises a future in which she will be able to enjoy both Love and Freedom together. Laughter in Schreiner's dream-world is not cynical but expressive of the energy and optimism that allows humanity to cling to the vision of the ideal against all experiential odds. One of Schreiner's earliest tales, 'The Hunter', extracted from *The Story of an African Farm*, offers us a gloss: the hunter, now almost at the end of his arduous and apparently unsuccessful search for Truth, wards off justifiable depression with laughter: 'He laughed fiercely; and the Echoes of despair slunk away, for the laugh of a brave strong heart is as a death-blow to them'.

By contrast, 'The Buddhist Priest's Wife' offers no such moment of transcendent hope precisely because its timescale is limited to the moment of lived suffering: 'the substance of it is that which I have lived all these years to learn, and suffered all that I have suffered to know'. Schreiner was probably right in thinking this 'much the best thing I have written' (Rive 208). For one thing, the interchange between the jocular, insensitive politician and the New Woman, shows an unexpected command of colloquial dialogue which lends a naturalistic surface to a highly-wrought symbolic tale. The walls of her rented room have been denuded of personal effects so that attention is repeatedly drawn to the last burning coals in the grate – a symbol of passion that she frequently re-used in her stories – and the slow dropping of cigarette-ash punctuating their final conversation. This companionable smoking in turn signifies a social emancipation that must preclude her from marrying a man whose political success is bound up in a life of men's clubs, male servants, and eventually identifying a wife, 'not too passionate' who will second his aims. The daring of inviting him to light his cigarette from her own stands proxy for the offer of a passion she cannot voice. For, despite the apparent frankness of their discussion of sexual difference, she remains convinced that a woman 'must always go with her arms folded sexually', never displaying her innermost feelings. These repeated somatic references make us almost unbearably aware of the repressed desire that he misreads as a disposition that will inevitably exclude her from being able 'to settle down and marry like other women'. The alternating tropes of exposure and concealment in which this story deals are signposted by an introductory command to 'cover' her dead body, now revealed as if upon a mortuary slab, and by the fable of the wounded stag which the woman tells in an attempt both to reveal and hide her own condition.

For modern readers there is a particularly puzzling moment in this tale, suggestive of a sensibility which we no longer share. Poised by the door to take their separate ways, the woman asks the man to kiss her. This he does, and 'in later years he could never tell certainly, but he always thought she put up her hand and rested it on the crown of his head, with a curious soft caress, something like a mother's touch when her child is asleep and she does not want to wake it'. Schreiner wills us to see in this the sublimation of the woman's desire into an expression of the highest moral state of which she believed women capable: motherhood. In *Women and Labour*, she wrote,

> It is this consciousness of great impersonal ends, to be brought, even if slowly and imperceptibly, a little nearer by her action, which gives to many a woman strength for renunciation, when she puts from her the lower type of sexual relationship ... if it offers her only enervation and parasitism; and which enables her often to accept poverty, toil, and sexual isolation ... and the renunciation of motherhood, that crowning beatitude of the woman's existence ... in the conviction that, by so doing, she makes more possible a fuller and higher attainment of motherhood and wifehood to the women who will follow her. (127)

It is easy to view her elevation of motherhood as unreconstructed patriarchal thinking, or as an idealisation born of a double lack: the absence of motherly love she felt in her own mother, and her own inability to become a mother. Making the unborn child, whose future the mother chooses in 'A Dream of Wild Bees', her ninth child – the position Schreiner herself occupied within the family – is suggestive of her need to assure herself that the maternal bond could be expressed in allowing the 'antenatal thing' its independent destiny. The repeated motif of renunciation, figured as a mother plucking the suckling child from her breast and giving it up to enable a greater good, in stories pre-dating her own series of miscarriages, points to a deep preoccupation with the allied themes of motherhood renounced and the sacrifice of the infant as a route to a greater good. The stark choices to be made on the colony's frontiers also played their role in shaping this motif: 'From my earliest years' she wrote in 'The Dawn of Civilisation', 'I had heard of bloodshed and battles and hairbreadth escapes'. In 1844 Schreiner's mother and her children had been forced to hide under a riverbank from a native attack and when she enjoined total silence on the group, that included the 3-week-old Ettie, Fred whispered to her, 'Mamma, Hadn't we better kill the baby?' (Cronwright-Schreiner 27). The folk-memories of the Long Trek, forming the background to 'Eighteen-ninety-nine', incorporate this tale, though with an interesting variation: here the child survives to bear three sons, each of whom dies, as does the genetic 'hope for the future', the much-loved grandson of this Boer family. Accounts that read this story as either a lament for women's suffering in war, or as contributing to the Boer myth of their loss of a promised land that is rightfully theirs, tend to miss the subtext. The grandmother-survivor is the story's wise woman, who prophesies that, according to the fortunes of political and economic ambition, the land will change hands repeatedly, but that 'This land will be a great land one day with one people from the sea to the north – but we shall not live to see it'. Accordingly the grandmother and her daughter resume tilling the land even when there are no direct descendants left. The true 'inheritors' are the Kaffir woman with the child at her breast who responds to other women's pain across the barriers of race and class, and the 'dead who lie quiet in their graves'.

The dedication to 'My Little Sister Ellie' of her novel, *From Man to Man* (1926) with the accompanying couplet,

> Nor knowest thou what argument
> Thy life to thy neighbour's creed hath lent

is further evidence of Schreiner's will to interpret the death, especially of the innocent, as establishing their role in mankind's future. Being named after three dead brothers may have made Schreiner feel that she too lived her life at others' expense. It was this belief in the contribution of the most insignificant individual to the Universe as a whole, articulated most clearly in 'The Dawn of Civilisation', that allowed her to see the strife 'to make that you hunger for real' worthwhile in the face of the depressing evidence of contemporary history and personal vicissitudes. It may also have prevented that young child, alone on the Karoo and feeling that 'the whole Universe seemed to be weighing down on me', from embracing the suicidal impulse of Thomas Hardy's Father Time, or subscribing to the degenerationist philosophy of many of her European contemporaries. Indeed it seems even to have enabled her to accept the suicides of close friends such as Eleanor Marx, or Amy Levy, with whom she had been on holiday only the week before, philosophically.

It also helped her to cope with her own childless state. 'The Artist's Secret', written when none of the relationships she contracted in England seemed likely to result in marriage and maternity, pictures the unique glow this artist achieved as the result of painting with his life-blood. Like the childless Virginia Woolf, who also spoke of having put 'my own life-blood into my writing', Schreiner spun for herself a version of the Victorian medical conviction that female artistic achievement might have to come at the price of reproduction (Lee 334).

Frequently Schreiner's discussions of 'the sex question' ring oddly to modern ears, accustomed to distinguish between biological identity and culturally-constructed gender, but in her beliefs about motherhood she was no essentialist: both 'The Policy in Favour of Protection—' and 'On the Banks of a Full River' make it clear that childless women can enjoy the privilege of 'mothering'. During the period in 1893 when she was considering whether to marry Cron, Schreiner admitted to him 'this power of absolute absorbing love for things beyond myself', which she identified with motherhood, had in her case become a fault, dissipating her sympathy 'as if I were the mother of everything that needs me'.

This 'uncontrollable outgoing to anything weak or in pain' (Rive 222) was also the key to her attitude to other women. The tale 'I Thought I Stood' stemmed from her involvement in the debate of the late 1880s about the role prostitutes perforce performed in protecting other more fortunate women. As the genesis of this tale indicates, however, befriending prostitutes came more easily than working together with her female peers. The tale ends by emphasising men and women's equal complicity in their fellow human beings' degradation, but the first part incorporates her immediate reaction to 'one of those infernal gatherings of women' she had just attended in London. A friend recalled how the following day Schreiner, 'striking her fist in her hand', had said, 'They talked about the degradation of women and the selfishness of men'; And then, after a pause, added, 'The selfishness of men and the selfishness of women – that is why I wrote this' (First and Scott 184).

Ideological disagreement, however, was not the sole source of Schreiner's frequent lack of sympathy for women of her own class. The emotional and physical intensity with which she argued her corner, combined with her total disregard for genteel dress codes, made her appear unconventional to the point of eccentricity, even, according to Cron, by South African standards. As a child she had a preference for going naked or wearing boys' clothes, and, in later life, roundly denounced the practice of wearing stays (Cronwright-Schreiner 68, 113 and 370). She was unprepared, however, for the disparaging comments and cold-shouldering her appearance would attract in Europe. During her stay in Alassio in 1888, she wrote to Edward Carpenter, 'Yesterday some of the women at the hotel laughed at my clothes and said at lunch that some people were too poor to afford proper dresses, etc., etc. I cried after I came out and I'm afraid they heard me, so I couldn't face them again today' (Rive 133). A few months later, her unaccompanied wanderings near the train station in Ventimiglia apparently led the Rev George MacDonald and his family to take her for a prostitute whom it was their duty to befriend (Rive 138). It is therefore unsurprising that her visions of the ideal often 'unclothe' humans to disclose to them their shared spiritual condition. The other side of this coin was the bitter contempt for handsomely dressed and richly bejewelled women, displayed in those stories that she set in realistic surroundings. Such concern for fine dress and furnishings, the coda tale to 'Eighteen-ninety-nine' suggests, was proof of callous blindness to the travails of the Empire that produced them. 'The Woman's Rose' delves a little more deeply into fashion's arbitrary preferences for the blonde over the brunette, or the newly modish over the familiar, presenting them as encoded into a patriarchally organised competition which pits one woman against another. It takes the generosity of another discarded beauty to teach her successor the compassionate stance of the 'mother heart' who can see all men as 'children'.

Frequently Schreiner's plots at first appear to work along the well-sanctioned lines of patriarchy: young girls, passionate in their sense of immediate personal injustice, receive counselling from older, wiser, women. However, these are not tales of socialisation: they insist, rather, that if education is to occur it will do so in the absence of men who, we are led to believe, would neither perceive nor understand the transaction, instigated by generous pity, that must take place between women before society can change. Tales such as 'The Policy in Favour of Protection—' and 'On the Banks of a Full River' are, in effect, tales of matriarchy in which men become the objects of desire that women must learn not to compete for, but to nurture. In her treatment of both the men and women whom Schreiner perceived as threatening her ideal society she had first to find a way of positioning them so that they should seem pitiable in their very blindness to the higher good.

Schreiner had, after all, attempted to pull the same trick on herself. Those tales that enjoy a fairly obvious autobiographical origin in her struggle to cling to her belief that 'the Universe is One' amid the sexual jealousy provoked by her unreciprocated love for Karl Pearson, process the hard-won triumph as an educational experience, relayed to a younger 'self' by a more mature friend, or omniscient spirit. From these tales of the split self Schreiner sought to mould a species of 'wisdom literature' for women. Strive as she might, however, to produce archetypal figures and an impersonal stance that would incorporate the passionate needs of the younger self and the sublimation of that passion into the older self's resolve to be 'the mother of everything that needs me', the result was often the same in her writing as in her life. As she told Cron, 'In fact this is the bad part of me, I lose control under the action of sympathy and do foolish things' (Rive 222). In literary terms this loss of control resulted in sentimentality. Tales which attempt to persuade us of the wisdom of universal benevolence are undermined by the venom with which younger women's selfishness is depicted and the way in which the odds are stacked against the older woman's happiness. Readers are prevented from endorsing the mature character's message of forgiveness by the raw sense of injustice that lingers in the presentation of her pain. Unlike the dream tales that arose from the same psychic wound, such as 'In a Ruined Chapel', the terrestrially-bound stories could provide no place for either prophetic assurance or self-transcending metamorphosis. By focusing on the drama between the man and the woman, rather than upon an internalised dispute between the split selves of womanhood, 'The Buddhist Priest's Wife' almost managed to maintain distance from the tale's victim, but the over-emphatic rhetoric employed by the disembodied, opening voice suggests how narrowly this voice teeters on a self-pitying fantasy of identification, in which the central woman character would herself envisage her premature death as precipitating a recognition of her true worth.

The introductory monologue to this tale functions as the obituary Schreiner would have wished for herself: 'She that had travelled so far, in so many lands, and done so much and seen so much, how she must like rest now!. The framing device, indeed, enacts the contrarieties at the heart of Schreiner's life and writing. The dignified silence of the Buddhist Priest's Wife's exit is, of course, undone, or offset, by recounting her story, just as the passionate complaints, voiced in Schreiner's many surviving letters to friends and relatives, both work against the image of the quiet, solitary, stoical self she fought for, and convey the extent of the idealism that believed such a transformation possible. In the very next paragraph of the letter in which she told her brother, Will, how this tale distilled both her life's suffering and 'all that I have suffered to know' she wrote:

> My legs are swollen and that always relieves my chest and head, but don't say anything about this to *anyone*. There is something so repulsive to me in disease; don't say anything to *anyone* .... (Rive 208)

The stories, dreams, and allegories in this volume bear witness to an intensely individual voice attempting always to transcend the merely personal through the forms and mask available to the artist. The task she set herself was to convey the vision of a child, born at the outpost of an Empire still ruled by 'the man with the gun' ('Dawn of Civilisation'), and to translate, for all her fellow human beings, the unquenchable hope of frontier existence that somewhere, just over the horizon, lay a place where a community founded on truth, justice and freedom could be realised. The distance she had been required to travel and the scale of her achievement is perhaps best conveyed by the reaction of a younger woman who met her towards the end of her life:

> There was a bitterness about her freethinking, I thought, which was not known to my generation; her battle had been hard and lonely, one guessed. We found our feet more easily because of the pioneering that had been done. (Cronwright-Schreiner 370)

Elisabeth Jay
Oxford Brookes University

# Works Cited and Further Reading

Asterisks denote criticism relevant to the contents of this volume.

Barash, Carol. *An Olive Schreiner Reader: Writings on Women and South Africa.* London: Pandora, 1987.*

Berkman, Joyce A. *The Healing Imagination of Olive Schreiner: Beyond South African Colonialism.* Amherst, Mass.: Massachusetts University Press, 1989.*

Burdett, Carolyn. *Olive Schreiner and the Progress of Feminism: Evolution, Gender, Empire.* Basingstoke: Palgrave, 2001.*

Clayton, Cherry. *Olive Schreiner.* New York & London: Twayne, Prentice Hall International, 1997. *

Clifford, James. 'On Ethnographic Self-Fashioning: Conrad and Malinowski.' *Writing Culture: The Poetics and Politics of Ethnography.* Ed. James Clifford and G. E. Marcus. Berkeley and London: University of California Press, 1986. 140–62.

Holland, Merlin and Rupert Hart-Davis, eds. *The Complete Letters of Oscar Wilde.* London: Fourth Estate, 2000.

Cronwright-Schreiner, Samuel C. *The Life of Olive Schreiner.* London: T. Fisher Unwin, 1924.

Donaldson, Laura E. *Decolonizing Feminisms: Race, Gender, and Empire-Building.* London: Routledge, 1992.*

Draznin, Yaffa C. *'My Other Self'* : *The Letters of Olive Schreiner and Havelock Ellis, 1884–1920.* New York: Peter Lang, 1992.

First, Ruth, and Ann Scott. *Olive Schreiner.* London: Andre Deutsch, 1980.*

Gilbert, Sandra M. and Susan Gubar. *No Man's Land: The Place of the Woman Writer in the Twentieth Century*, Volume 1: *The War of the Words.* New Haven and London: Yale University Press, 1987.*

Horton, Susan R. *Difficult Women, Artful Lives: Olive Schreiner and Isak Dinesen, In and Out of Africa.* London and Baltimore: Johns Hopkins University Press, 1995.

Joyce, James. *A Portrait of the Artist as a Young Man.* 1916. London: Penguin, 1967.

Lawrence, D. H. *The Rainbow.* 1915. London: Heinemann, 1977.

Lee, Hermione. *Virginia Woolf.* London: Chatto and Windus, 1996.

McCracken, Scott. 'Stages of Sand and Blood: the Performance of Gendered Subjectivity in Olive Schreiner's Colonial Allegories.' *Rereading Victorian Fiction.* Ed. Alice Jenkins and Juliet John. Basingstoke: Palgrave, 2000. 145–58.*

Rive, Richard, ed. *Olive Schreiner Letters*, Volume I: *1871–1889.* Oxford: Oxford University Press, 1988.

Schreiner, Olive. *From Man to Man.* London: T. Fisher Unwin, 1926.

—— *Woman and Labour.* London: T. Fisher Unwin, 1911.

Showalter, Elaine. *A Literature of their Own: British Women Novelists from Charlotte Brontë to Doris Lessing.* London: Virago, 1984.*

—— *Sexual Anarchy: Gender and Culture at the Fin de Siècle.* 1992. London: Virago 1995.*

Walkowitz, Judith R. 'Science, Feminism, and Romance: The Men and Women's Club, 1885-1889.' *History Workshop Journal* 21 (1986): 37–59.

Worthen, John. *D. H. Lawrence: The Early Years, 1885–1912.* Cambridge: Cambridge University Press, 1991.

Woolf, Virginia. 'Olive Schreiner.' *The New Republic* 18 March 1925. *The Essays of Virginia Woolf.* Volume 4. *1925–1928.* Ed. Andrew McNeillie. London: Hogarth Press, 1994: 4–6.

—— *Three Guineas.* 1938. Oxford: Oxford University Press, 1992.

# A Note on the Text

This book forms the first compendium of all three collections of Schreiner's dreams, stories and allegories. In each case this text follows the second edition.

The second edition of *Dreams* (1891) added a page, bearing Schreiner's portrait, to the first edition of 1890. The second edition, published in 1924, of *Stories, Dreams and Allegories* (1923) added 'The Dawn of Civilisation'. When she published *Dreams* Schreiner was at pains to explain that the ordering of the volume followed the order of composition: this collection has therefore retained both the internal and volume sequencing of the original editions.

The posthumous editing of *Stories, Dreams and Allegories* by Schreiner's widower, aided by her old friend, Havelock Ellis, requires a little further comment. In his Preface to the collection Cron claimed that the previously unpublished pieces 'appeared unaltered, except in a few minor respects like punctuation, as I found them among her papers' (Schreiner's spelling and punctuation were notably erratic). However, in his Introductory essay to her incomplete novel *From Man to Man* (1926) Cron described the rather more interventionist editorial process necessitated by Schreiner's habit of continual revision:

> ... there were three drafts of *The Buddhist Priest's Wife*, each progressively shorter than the previous one and none of them quite complete; to get the final draft I had to sort out the last two drafts in several ways – by handwriting, by age of the paper, and so on,– then get the (often wrongly-numbered) sheets into consecutive order respectively, then compare and adjust them. It was much the same with *On the Banks of a Full River*, and with several of her other writings (14).

In every instance where information exists as to publication of individual pieces, prior to their publication in volume form, this text notes this at the conclusion of the relevant tale.

The explanatory notes to South African terms, considered necessary by Schreiner, have been retained within the main body of the text: a brief additional glossary will be found at the end of the book.

# DREAMS

**To
A SMALL GIRL-CHILD,**
WHO MAY LIVE TO GRASP
SOMEWHAT OF THAT WHICH FOR US
IS YET SIGHT, NOT TOUCH

### NOTE.

*THESE* Dreams are printed in the order in which they were written.
*In the case of two there was a lapse of some years between the writing of the first
and last parts; these are placed according to the date of the first part.*

*OLIVE SCHREINER.*

MATJESFONTEIN
CAPE COLONY
SOUTH AFRICA
*November, 1890*

# I
# The Lost Joy

All day, where the sunlight played on the sea-shore, Life sat.

All day the soft wind played with her hair, and the young, young face looked out across the water. She was waiting – she was waiting; but she could not tell for what.

All day the waves ran up and up on the sand, and ran back again, and the pink shells rolled. Life sat waiting; all day, with the sunlight in her eyes, she sat there, till, grown weary, she laid her head upon her knee and fell asleep, waiting still.

Then a keel grated on the sand, and then a step was on the shore – Life awoke and heard it. A hand was laid upon her, and a great shudder passed through her. She looked up, and saw over her the strange, wide eyes of Love – and Life now knew for whom she had sat there waiting.

And Love drew Life up to him.

And of that meeting was born a thing rare and beautiful – Joy, First-Joy was it called. The sunlight when it shines upon the merry water is not so glad; the rosebuds, when they turn back their lips for the sun's first kiss, are not so ruddy. Its tiny pulses beat quick. It was so warm, so soft! It never spoke, but it laughed and played in the sunshine: and Love and Life rejoiced exceedingly. Neither whispered it to the other, but deep in its own heart each said, "It shall be ours for ever."

Then there came a time – was it after weeks? was it after months? (Love and Life do not measure time) – when the thing was not as it had been.

Still it played; still it laughed; still it stained its mouth with purple berries; but sometimes the little hands hung weary, and the little eyes looked out heavily across the water.

And Life and Love dared not look into each other's eyes, dared not say, "What ails our darling?" Each heart whispered to itself, "It is nothing, it is nothing, to-morrow it will laugh out clear." But to-morrow and to-morrow came. They journeyed on, and the child played beside them, but heavily, more heavily.

One day Life and Love lay down to sleep; and when they awoke, it was gone: only, near them, on the grass, sat a little stranger, with wide-open eyes, very soft and sad. Neither noticed it; but they walked apart, weeping bitterly, "Oh, our Joy! our lost Joy! shall we see you no more for ever?"

The little soft and sad-eyed stranger slipped a hand into one hand of each, and drew them closer, and Life and Love walked on with it between them. And when Life looked down in anguish, she saw her tears reflected in its soft eyes. And when Love, mad with pain, cried out, "I am weary, I am weary! I can journey no further. The light is all behind, the dark is all before," a little rosy finger pointed where the sunlight lay upon the hill- sides. Always its large eyes were sad and thoughtful: always the little brave mouth was smiling quietly.

When on the sharp stones Life cut her feet, he wiped the blood upon his garments, and kissed the wounded feet with his little lips. When in the desert Love lay down faint (for Love itself grows faint), he ran over the hot sand with his little naked feet, and even there in the desert found water in the holes in the rocks to moisten Love's lips with. He was no burden – he never weighted them; he only helped them forward on their journey.

When they came to the dark ravine where the icicles hang from the rocks – for Love and Life must pass through strange drear places – there, where all is cold, and the snow lies thick, he took their freezing hands and held them against his beating little heart, and warmed them – and softly he drew them on and on.

And when they came beyond, into the land of sunshine and flowers, strangely the great eyes lit up, and dimples broke out upon the face. Brightly laughing, it ran over the soft grass; gathered honey from the hollow tree; and brought it them on the palm of its hand; carried them water in the leaves of the lily, and gathered flowers and wreathed them round their heads, softly laughing all the while. He touched them as their Joy had touched them, but his fingers clung more tenderly.

So they wandered on, through the dark lands and the light, always with that little brave smiling one between them. Sometimes they remembered that first radiant Joy, and whispered to themselves, "Oh! could we but find him also!"

At last they came to where Reflection sits; that strange old woman who has always one elbow on her knee, and her chin in her hand, and who steals light out of the past to shed it on the future.

And Life and Love cried out, "O wise one! tell us: when first we met, a lovely radiant thing belonged to us – gladness without a tear, sunshine without a shade. Oh! how did we sin that we lost it? Where shall we go that we may find it?"

And she, the wise old woman, answered, "To have it back, will you give up that which walks beside you now?"

And in agony Love and Life cried, "No!"

"Give up this!" said Life. "When the thorns have pierced me, who will suck the poison out? When my head throbs, who will lay his tiny hands upon it and still the beating? In the cold and the dark, who will warm my freezing heart?"

And Love cried out, "Better let me die! Without Joy I can live; without this I cannot. Let me rather die, not lose it!"

And the wise old woman answered, "O fools and blind! What you once had is that which you have now! When Love and Life first meet, a radiant thing is born, without a shade. When the roads begin to roughen, when the shades begin to darken, when the days are hard, and the nights cold and long – then it begins to change. Love and Life *will* not see it, *will* not know it – till one day they start up suddenly, crying, 'O God! O God! we have lost it! Where is it?' They do not understand that they could not carry the laughing thing unchanged into the desert, and the frost, and the snow. They do not know that what walks beside them still is the Joy grown older. The grave, sweet, tender thing – warm in the coldest snows, brave in the dreariest deserts – its name is Sympathy; it is the Perfect Love."

*South Africa.*

First published in *The Woman's World*, edited by Oscar Wilde, September 1888.

# II
# The Hunter

In certain valleys there was a hunter. Day by day he went to hunt for wild-fowl in the woods; and it chanced that once he stood on the shores of a large lake. While he stood waiting in the rushes for the coming of the birds, a great shadow fell on him, and in the water he saw a reflection. He looked up to the sky; but the thing was gone. Then a burning desire came over him to see once again that reflection in the water, and all day he watched and waited; but night came and it had not returned. Then he went home with his empty bag, moody and silent. His comrades came questioning about him to know the reason, but he answered them nothing; he sat alone and brooded. Then his friend came to him, and to him he spoke.

"I have seen to-day," he said, "that which I never saw before – a vast white bird, with silver wings outstretched, sailing in the everlasting blue. And now it is as though a great fire burnt within my breast. It was but a sheen, a shimmer, a reflection in the water; but now I desire nothing more on earth than to hold her."

His friend laughed.

"It was but a beam playing on the water, or the shadow of your own head. To-morrow you will forget her," he said.

But to-morrow, and to-morrow, and to-morrow the hunter walked alone. He sought in the forest and in the woods, by the lakes and among the rushes, but he could not find her. He shot no more wild fowl; what were they to him?

"What ails him?" said his comrades.

"He is mad," said one.

"No; but he is worse," said another; "he would see that which none of us have seen, and make himself a wonder."

"Come, let us forswear his company," said all.

So the hunter walked alone.

One night, as he wandered in the shade, very heartsore and weeping, an old man stood before him, grander and taller than the sons of men.

"Who are you?" asked the hunter.

"I am Wisdom," answered the old man; "but some men call me Knowledge. All my life I have grown in these valleys; but no man sees me till he has sorrowed much. The eyes must be washed with tears that are to behold me; and, according as a man has suffered, I speak."

And the hunter cried–

"Oh, you who have lived here so long, tell me, what is that great wild bird I have seen sailing in the blue? They would have me believe she is a dream; the shadow of my own head."

The old man smiled.

"Her name is Truth. He who has once seen her never rests again. Till death he desires her."

And the hunter cried–

"Oh, tell me where I may find her."

But the man said:

"You have not suffered enough," and went.

Then the hunter took from his breast the shuttle of Imagination, and wound on it the thread of his Wishes; and all night he sat and wove a net.

In the morning he spread the golden net upon the ground, and into it he threw a few grains of credulity, which his father had left him, and which he kept in his breast-pocket. They were like white puff-balls, and when you trod on them a brown dust flew out. Then he sat by to see what would happen. The first that came into the net was a snow-white bird, with dove's eyes, and he sang a beautiful song – "A human-God! a human-God! a human-God!" it sang. The second that came was black and mystical, with dark, lovely eyes, that looked into the depths of your soul, and he sang only this – "Immortality!"

And the hunter took them both in his arms, for he said –

"They are surely of the beautiful family of Truth."

Then came another, green and gold, who sang in a shrill voice, like one crying in the marketplace, – "Reward after Death! Reward after Death!"

And he said –

"You are not so fair; but you are fair too," and he took it.

And others came, brightly coloured, singing pleasant songs, till all the grains were finished. And the hunter gathered all his birds together, and built a strong iron cage called a new creed, and put all his birds in it.

Then the people came about dancing and singing.

"Oh, happy hunter!" they cried. "Oh, wonderful man! Oh, delightful birds! Oh, lovely songs!"

No one asked where the birds had come from, nor how they had been caught; but they danced and sang before them. And the hunter too was glad, for he said–

"Surely Truth is among them. In time she will moult her feathers, and I shall see her snow-white form."

But the time passed, and the people sang and danced; but the hunter's heart grew heavy. He crept alone, as of old, to weep; the terrible desire had awakened again in his breast. One day, as he sat alone weeping, it chanced that Wisdom met him. He told the old man what he had done.

And Wisdom smiled sadly.

"Many men," he said, "have spread that net for Truth; but they have never found her. On the grains of credulity she will not feed; in the net of wishes her feet cannot be held; in the air of these valleys she will not breathe. The birds you have caught are of the brood of Lies. Lovely and beautiful, but still lies; Truth knows them not."

And the hunter cried out in bitterness –

"And must I then sit still to be devoured of this great burning?"

And the old man said,

"Listen, and in that you have suffered much and wept much, I will tell you what I know. He who sets out to search for Truth must leave these valleys of superstition for ever, taking with him not one shred that has belonged to them. Alone he must wander down into the Land of Absolute Negation and Denial; he must abide there; he must resist temptation; when the light breaks he must arise and follow it into the country of dry sunshine. The mountains of stern reality will rise before him; he must climb them; *beyond* them lies Truth."

"And he will hold her fast! he will hold her in his hands!" the hunter cried.

Wisdom shook his head.

"He will never see her, never hold her. The time is not yet."

"Then there is no hope?" cried the hunter.

"There is this," said Wisdom: "Some men have climbed on those mountains; circle above circle of bare rock they have scaled; and, wandering there, in those high regions, some have chanced to pick up on the ground one white, silver feather, dropped from the wing of Truth. And it shall come to pass," said the old man, raising himself prophetically and pointing with his finger to the sky, "it shall come to pass, that when enough of those silver feathers shall have been gathered by the hands of men, and shall have been woven into a cord, and the cord into a net, that in *that* net Truth may be captured. *Nothing but Truth can hold Truth.*"

The hunter arose. "I will go," he said.

But wisdom detained him.

"Mark you well – who leaves these valleys *never* returns to them. Though he should weep tears of blood seven days and nights upon the confines, he can never put his foot across them. Left – they are left for ever. Upon the road which you would travel there is no reward offered. Who goes, goes freely – for the great love that is in him. The work is his reward."

"I go" said the hunter; "but upon the mountains, tell me, which path shall I take?"

"I am the child of The-Accumulated-Knowledge-of-Ages," said the man; "I can walk only where many men have trodden. On these mountains few feet have passed; each man strikes out a path for himself. He goes at his own peril: my voice he hears no more. I may follow after him, but I cannot go before him."

Then Knowledge vanished.

And the hunter turned. He went to his cage, and with his hands broke down the bars, and the jagged iron tore his flesh. It is sometimes easier to build than to break.

One by one he took his plumed birds and let them fly. But when he came to his dark-plumed bird, he held it, and looked into its beautiful eyes, and the bird uttered its low deep cry – "Immortality!"

And he said quickly: "I cannot part with it. It is not heavy; it eats no food. I will hide it in my breast; I will take it with me." And he buried it there and covered it over with his cloak.

But the thing he had hidden grew heavier, heavier, heavier – till it lay on his breast like lead. He could not move with it. He could not leave those valleys with it. Then again he took it out and looked at it.

"Oh, my beautiful! my heart's own!" he cried, "may I not keep you?"

He opened his hands sadly.

"Go!" he said. "It may happen that in Truth's song one note is like to yours; but *I* shall never hear it."

Sadly he opened his hand, and the bird flew from him for ever.

Then from the shuttle of Imagination he took the thread of his wishes, and threw it on the ground; and the empty shuttle he put into his breast, for the thread was made in those valleys, but the shuttle came from an unknown country. He turned to go, but now the people came about him, howling.

"Fool, hound, demented lunatic!" they cried. "How dared you break your cage and let the birds fly?'

The hunter spoke; but they would not hear him.

"Truth! who is she? Can you eat her? can you drink her? Who has ever seen her? Your birds were real: all could hear them sing! Oh, fool! vile reptile! atheist!" they cried, "you pollute the air."

"Come, let us take up stones and stone him," cried some.

"What affair is it of ours?" said others. "Let the idiot go," and went away. But the rest gathered up stones and mud and threw at him. At last, when he was bruised and cut, the hunter crept away into the woods. And it was evening about him.

He wandered on and on, and the shade grew deeper. He was on the borders now of the land where it is always night. Then he stepped into it, and there was no light there. With his hands he groped; but each branch as he touched it broke off, and the earth was covered with cinders. At every step his foot sank in, and a fine cloud of impalpable ashes flew up into his face; and it was dark. So he sat down upon a stone and buried his face in his hands, to wait in that Land of Negation and Denial till the light came.

And it was night in his heart also.

Then from the marshes to his right and left cold mists arose and closed about him. A fine, imperceptible rain fell in the dark, and great drops gathered on his hair and clothes. His heart beat slowly, and a numbness crept through all his limbs. Then, looking up, two merry wisp lights came dancing. He lifted his head to look at them. Nearer, nearer they came. So warm, so bright, they danced like stars of fire. They stood before him at last. From the centre of the radiating flame in one looked out a woman's face, laughing, dimpled, with streaming yellow hair. In the centre of the other were merry laughing ripples, like the bubbles on a glass of wine. They danced before him.

"Who are you," asked the hunter, "who alone come to me in my solitude and darkness?"

"We are the twins Sensuality," they cried. "Our father's name is Human-Nature, and our mother's name is Excess. We are as old as the hills and rivers, as old as the first man; but we never die," they laughed.

"Oh, let me wrap my arms about you!" cried the first; "they are soft and warm. Your heart is frozen now, but I will make it beat. Oh, come to me!"

"I will pour my hot life into you," said the second; "your brain is numb, and your limbs are dead now; but they shall live with a fierce free life. Oh, let me pour it in!"

"Oh, follow us," they cried, "and live with us. Nobler hearts than yours have sat here in this darkness to wait, and they have come to us and we to them; and they have never left us, never. All else is a delusion, but *we* are real, we are real. Truth is a shadow; the valleys of superstition are a farce: the earth is of ashes, the trees all rotten; but we – feel us – we live! You cannot doubt us. Feel us, how warm we are! Oh, come to us! Come with us!"

Nearer and nearer round his head they hovered, and the cold drops melted on his forehead. The bright light shot into his eyes, dazzling him, and the frozen blood began to run. And he said–

"Yes, why should I die here in this awful darkness? They are warm, they melt my frozen blood!" and he stretched out his hands to take them.

Then in a moment there arose before him the image of the thing he had loved, and his hand dropped to his side.

"Oh, come to us!" they cried.

But he buried his face.

"You dazzle my eyes," he cried, "you make my heart warm; but you cannot give me what I desire. I will wait here – wait till I die. Go!"

He covered his face with his hands and would not listen; and when he looked up again they were two twinkling stars, that vanished in the distance.

And the long, long night rolled on.

All who leave the valley of superstition pass through that dark land; but some go through it in a few days, some linger there for months, some for years, and some die there.

At last for the hunter a faint light played along the horizon, and he rose to follow it; and he reached that light at last, and stepped into the broad sunshine. Then before him rose the almighty mountains of Dry-facts and Realities. The clear sunshine played on them, and the tops were lost in the clouds. At the foot many paths ran up. An exultant cry burst from the hunter. He chose the straightest and began to climb; and the rocks and ridges resounded with his song. They had exaggerated; after all, it was not so high, nor was the road so steep! A few days, a few weeks, a few months at most, and then the top! Not one feather only would he pick up; he would gather all that other men had found – weave the net – capture Truth – hold her fast – touch her with his hands – clasp her!

He laughed in the merry sunshine, and sang loud. Victory was very near. Nevertheless, after a while the path grew steeper. He needed all his breath for climbing, and the singing died away. On the right and left rose huge rocks, devoid of lichen or moss, and in the lava-like earth chasms yawned. Here and there he saw a sheen of white bones. Now too the path began to grow less and less marked; then it became a mere trace, with a foot-mark here and there; then it ceased altogether. He sang no more, but struck forth a path for himself, until he reached a mighty wall of rock, smooth and without break, stretching as far as the eye could see. "I will rear a stair against it; and, once this wall climbed, I shall be almost there," he said bravely; and worked. With his shuttle of imagination he dug out stones; but half of them would not fit, and half a month's work would roll down because those below were ill chosen. But the hunter worked on, saying always to himself, "Once this wall climbed, I shall be almost there. This great work ended!"

At last he came out upon the top, and he looked about him. Far below rolled the white mist over the valleys of superstition, and above him towered the mountains. They had seemed low before; they were of an immeasurable height now, from crown to foundation surrounded by walls of rock, that rose tier above tier in mighty circles. Upon them played the eternal sunshine. He uttered a wild cry. He bowed himself on to the earth, and when he rose his face was white. In absolute silence he walked on. He was very silent now. In those high regions the rarefied air is hard to breathe by those born in the valleys; every breath he drew hurt him, and the blood oozed out from the tips of his fingers. Before the next wall of rock he began to work. The height of this seemed infinite, and he said nothing. The sound of his tool rang night and day upon the iron rocks into which he cut steps. Years passed over him, yet he worked on; but the wall towered up always above him to heaven. Sometimes he prayed that a little moss or lichen might spring up on those bare walls to be a companion to him; but it never came.

And the years rolled on; he counted them by the steps he had cut – a few for a year – only a few. He sang no more; he said no more, "I will do this or that" – he only worked. And at night, when the twilight settled down, there looked out at him from the holes and crevices in the rocks strange wild faces.

"Stop your work, you lonely man, and speak to us," they cried.

"My salvation is in work. If I should stop but for one moment you would creep down upon me," he replied. And they put out their long necks further.

"Look down into the crevice at your feet," they said. "See what lie there - - white bones! As brave and strong a man as you climbed to these rocks. And he looked up. He saw there was no use in striving; he would never hold Truth, never see her, never find her. So he lay down here, for he was very tired. He went to sleep forever. He put himself to sleep. Sleep is very tranquil. You are not lonely when you are asleep, neither do your hands ache, nor your heart." And the hunter laughed between his teeth.

"Have I torn from my heart all that was dearest; have I wandered alone in the land of night; have I resisted temptation; have I dwelt where the voice of my kind is never heard, and laboured alone, to lie down and be food for you, ye harpies?"

He laughed fiercely; and the Echoes of Despair slunk away, for the laugh of a brave, strong heart is as a death-blow to them.

Nevertheless they crept out again and looked at him.

"Do you know that your hair is white?" they said, "that your hands begin to tremble like a child's? Do you see that the point of your shuttle is gone? – it is cracked already. If you should ever climb this stair," they said, "it will be your last. You will never climb another."

And he answered, "*I know it!*" and worked on.

The old, thin hands cut the stones ill and jaggedly, for the fingers were stiff and bent. The beauty and the strength of the man was gone.

At last, an old, wizened, shrunken face looked out above the rocks. It saw the eternal mountains rise with walls to the white clouds; but its work was done.

The old hunter folded his tired hands and lay down by the precipice where he had worked away his life. It was the sleeping time at last. Below him over the valleys rolled the thick white mist. Once it broke; and through the gap the dying eyes looked down on the trees and fields of their childhood. From afar seemed borne to him the cry of his own wild birds, and he heard the noise of people singing as they danced. And he thought he heard among them the voices of his old comrades; and he saw far off the sunlight shine on his early home. And great tears gathered in the hunter's eyes.

"Ah! they who die there do not die alone," he cried.

Then the mists rolled together again; and he turned his eyes away.

"I have sought," he said, "for long years I have laboured; but I have not found her. I have not rested, I have not repined, and I have not seen her; now my strength is gone. Where I lie down worn out ,other men will stand, young and fresh. By the steps that I have cut they will climb; by the stairs that I have built, they will mount. They will never know the name of the man who made them. At the clumsy work they will laugh; when the stones roll they will curse me. But they will mount, and on *my* work; they will climb, and by *my* stair! They will find her, and through me! And no man liveth to himself, and no man dieth to himself."

The tears rolled from beneath the shrivelled eyelids. If Truth had appeared above him in the clouds now he could not have seen her, the mist of death was in his eyes.

"My soul hears their glad step coming," he said; "and they shall mount! they shall mount!" He raised his shrivelled hand to his eyes.

Then slowly from the white sky above, through the still air, came something falling, falling, falling. Softly it fluttered down, and dropped on to the breast of the dying man. He felt it with his hands. It was a feather. He died holding it.

First published in Schreiner's novel *The Story of an African Farm* (1883). A few minor cuts were made to loosen this tale from its original context, where it served as a commentary on Waldo's rudimentary carving and the artist's vocation.

# III
# The Gardens of Pleasure

She walked upon the beds, and the sweet rich scent arose; and she gathered her hands full of flowers. Then Duty, with his white clear features, came and looked at her. Then she ceased from gathering, but she walked away among the flowers, smiling, and with her hands full.

Then Duty, with his still white face, came again, and looked at her; but she, she turned her head away from him. At last she saw his face, and she dropped the fairest of the flowers she had held, and walked silently away.

Then again he came to her. And she moaned, and bent her head low, and turned to the gate. But as she went out she looked back at the sunlight on the faces of the flowers, and wept in anguish. Then she went out, and it shut behind her for ever; but still in her hand she held of the buds she had gathered, and the scent was very sweet in the lonely desert.

But he followed her. Once more he stood before her with his still, white, death-like face. And she knew what he had come for: she unbent the fingers, and let the flowers drop out, the flowers she had loved so, and walked on without them, with dry, aching eyes. Then for the last time he came. And she showed him her empty hands, the hands that held nothing now. But still he looked. Then at length she opened her bosom and took out of it one small flower she had hidden there, and laid it on the sand. She had nothing more to give now, and she wandered away, and the grey sand whirled about her.

# IV
# In a Far-Off World

There is a world in one of the far-off stars, and things do not happen here as they happen there.

In that world were a man and woman; they had one work, and they walked together side by side on many days, and were friends – and that is a thing that happens now and then in this world also.

But there was something in that star-world that there is not here. There was a thick wood: where the trees grew closest, and the stems were interlocked, and the summer sun never shone, there stood a shrine. In the day all was quiet, but at night, when the stars shone or the moon glinted on the tree-tops, and all was quiet below, if one crept here quite alone and knelt on the steps of the stone altar, and uncovering one's breast, so wounded it that the blood fell down on the altar steps, then whatever he who knelt there wished for was granted him. And all this happens, as I said, because it is a far-off world, and things often happen there as they do not happen here.

Now, the man and woman walked together; and the woman wished well to the man. One night when the moon was shining so that the leaves of all the trees glinted, and the waves of the sea were silvery, the woman walked alone to the forest. It was dark there; the moonlight fell only in little flecks on the dead leaves under her feet, and the branches were knotted tight overhead. Farther in it got darker, not even a fleck of moonlight shone. Then she came to the shrine; she knelt down before it and prayed; there came no answer. Then she uncovered her breast; with a sharp two-edged stone that lay there she wounded it. The drops dripped slowly down on to the stone, and a voice cried, "What do you seek?"

She answered, "There is a man; I hold him nearer than anything. I would give him the best of all blessings."

The voice said, "What is it?"

The girl said, "I know not, but that which is most good for him I wish him to have."

The voice said, "Your prayer is answered; he shall have it."

Then she stood up. She covered her breast and held the garment tight upon it with her hand, and ran out of the forest, and the dead leaves fluttered under her feet. Out in the moonlight the soft air was blowing, and the sand glittered on the beach. She ran along the smooth shore, then suddenly she stood still. Out across the water there was something moving. She shaded her eyes and looked. It was a boat; it was sliding swiftly over the moonlit water out to sea. One stood upright in it; the face the moonlight did not show, but the figure she knew. It was passing swiftly; it seemed as if no one propelled it; the moonlight's shimmer did not let her see clearly, and the boat was far from shore, but it seemed almost as if there was another figure sitting in the stern. Faster and faster it glided over the water away, away. She ran along the shore; she came no nearer it. The garment she had held closed fluttered open; she stretched out her arms, and the moonlight shone on her long loose hair.

Then a voice beside her whispered, "What is it?"

She cried, "With my blood I bought the best of all gifts for him. I have come to bring it him! He is going from me!"

The voice whispered softly, "Your prayer was answered. It has been given him."

She cried, "What is it?"

The voice answered, "It is that he might leave you."

The girl stood still.

Far out at sea the boat was lost to sight beyond the moonlight sheen.

The voice spoke softly, "Art thou contented?"

She said, "I am contented."

At her feet the waves broke in long ripples softly on the shore.

# V
# Three Dreams in a Desert

### Under a Mimosa-Tree

As I travelled across an African plain the sun shone down hotly. Then I drew my horse up under a mimosa-tree, and I took the saddle from him and left him to feed among the parched bushes. And all to right and to left stretched the brown earth. And I sat down under the tree, because the heat beat fiercely, and all along the horizon the air throbbed. And after a while a heavy drowsiness came over me, and I laid my head down against my saddle, and I fell asleep there. And, in my sleep, I had a curious dream.

I thought I stood on the border of a great desert, and the sand blew about everywhere. And I thought I saw two great figures like beasts of burden of the desert, and one lay upon the sand with its neck stretched out, and one stood by it. And I looked curiously at the one that lay upon the ground, for it had a great burden on its back, and the sand was thick about it, so that it seemed to have piled over it for centuries.

And I looked very curiously at it. And there stood one beside me watching. And I said to him, "What is this huge creature who lies here on the sand?"

And he said, "This is woman; she that bears men in her body."

And I said, "Why does she lie here motionless with the sand piled round her?"

And he answered, "Listen, I will tell you! Ages and ages long she has lain here, and the wind has blown over her. The oldest, oldest, oldest man living has never seen her move: the oldest, oldest book records that she lay here then, as she lies here now, with the sand about her. But listen! Older than the oldest book, older than the oldest recorded memory of man, on the Rocks of Language, on the hard-baked clay of Ancient Customs, now crumbling to decay, are found the marks of her footsteps! Side by side with his who stands beside her you may trace them; and you know that she who now lies there once wandered free over the rocks with him."

And I said, "Why does she lie there now?"

And he said, "I take it, ages ago the Age-of-dominion-of-muscular-force found her, and when she stooped low to give suck to her young, and her back was broad, he put his burden of subjection on to it, and tied it on with the broad band of Inevitable Necessity. Then she looked at the earth and the sky, and knew there was no hope for her; and she lay down on the sand with the burden she could not loosen. Ever since she has lain here. And the ages have come, and the ages have gone, but the band of Inevitable Necessity has not been cut."

And I looked and saw in her eyes the terrible patience of the centuries; the ground was wet with her tears, and her nostrils blew up the sand.

And I said, "Has she ever tried to move?"

And he said, "Sometimes a limb has quivered. But she is wise; she knows she cannot rise with the burden on her."

And I said, "Why does not he who stands by her leave her and go on?"

And he said, "He cannot. Look – "

And I saw a broad band passing along the ground from one to the other, and it bound them together.

He said, "While she lies there he must stand and look across the desert."

And I said, "Does he know why he cannot move?"

And he said, "No."

And I heard a sound of something cracking, and I looked, and I saw the band that bound the burden on to her back broken asunder; and the burden rolled on to the ground.

And I said, "What is this?"

And he said, "The Age-of-muscular-force is dead. The Age-of-nervous-force has killed him with the knife he holds in his hand; and silently and invisibly he has crept up to the woman, and with that knife of Mechanical Invention he has cut the band that bound the burden to her back. The Inevitable Necessity is broken. She might rise now."

And I saw that she still lay motionless on the sand, with her eyes open and her neck stretched out. And she seemed to look for something on the far-off border of the desert that never came. And I wondered if she were awake or asleep. And as I looked her body quivered, and a light came into her eyes, like when a sunbeam breaks into a dark room.

I said, "What is it?"

He whispered "Hush! the thought has come to her, 'Might I not rise?'"

And I looked. And she raised her head from the sand, and I saw the dent where her neck had lain so long. And she looked at the earth, and she looked at the sky, and she looked at him who stood by her: but he looked out across the desert.

And I saw her body quiver; and she pressed her front knees to the earth, and veins stood out; and I cried; "She is going to rise!"

But only her sides heaved, and she lay still where she was.

But her head she held up; she did not lay it down again. And he beside me said, "She is very weak. See, her legs have been crushed under her so long."

And I saw the creature struggle: and the drops stood out on her.

And I said, "Surely he who stands beside her will help her?"

And he beside me answered, "He cannot help her: *she must help herself. Let her struggle till she is strong.*"

And I cried, "At least he will not hinder her! See, he moves farther from her, and tightens the cord between them, and he drags her down."

And he answered, "He does not understand. When she moves she draws the band that binds them, and hurts him, and he moves farther from her. The day will come when he will understand, and will know what she is doing. Let her once stagger on to her knees. In that day he will stand close to her, and look into her eyes with sympathy."

And she stretched her neck, and the drops fell from her. And the creature rose an inch from the earth and sank back.

And I cried, "Oh, she is too weak! she cannot walk! The long years have taken all her strength from her. Can she never move?"

And he answered me, "See the light in her eyes!"

And slowly the creature staggered on to its knees.

And I awoke: and all to the east and to the west stretched the barren earth, with the dry bushes on it. The ants ran up and down in the red sand, and the heat beat fiercely. I looked up through the thin branches of the tree at the blue sky overhead. I stretched myself, and I mused over the dream I had had. And I fell asleep again, with my head on my saddle. And in the fierce heat I had another dream.

I saw a desert and I saw a woman coming out of it. And she came to the bank of a dark river; and the bank was steep and high.[1] And on it an old man met her, who had a long white beard; and a stick that curled was in his hand, and on it was written Reason. And he asked her what she wanted; and she said "I am woman; and I am seeking for the land of Freedom."

And he said, "It is before you."

And she said, "I see nothing before me but a dark flowing river, and a bank steep and high, and cuttings here and there with heavy sand in them."

And he said, "And beyond that?"

She said, "I see nothing, but sometimes, when I shade my eyes with my hand, I think I see on the further bank trees and hills, and the sun shining on them!"

He said, "That is the Land of Freedom."

She said, "How am I to get there?"

He said, "There is one way, and one only. Down the banks of Labour, through the water of Suffering. There is no other."

She said, "Is there no bridge?"

He answered, "None."

She said, "Is the water deep?"

He said, "Deep."

She said, "Is the floor worn?"

He said, "It is. Your foot may slip at any time, and you may be lost."

She said, "Have any crossed already?"

He said, "Some have *tried*!"

---

1. The banks of an African river are sometimes a hundred feet high, and consist of deep shifting sands, through which in the course of ages the river has worn its gigantic bed.

She said, "Is there a track to show where the best fording is?"

He said, "It has to be made."

She shaded her eyes with her hand; and she said, "I will go."

And he said, "You must take off the clothes you wore in the desert: they are dragged down by them who go into the water so clothed."

And she threw from her gladly the mantle of Ancient-received-opinions she wore, for it was worn full of holes. And she took the girdle from her waist that she had treasured so long, and the moths flew out of it in a cloud. And he said, "Take the shoes of dependence off your feet."

And she stood there naked, but for one white garment that clung close to her.

And he said, "That you may keep. So they wear clothes in the Land of Freedom. In the water it buoys; it always swims."

And I saw on its breast was written Truth; and it was white; the sun had not often shone on it; the other clothes had covered it up. And he said, "Take this stick; hold it fast. In that day when it slips from your hand you are lost. Put it down before you; feel your way: where it cannot find a bottom do not set your foot."

And she said, "I am ready; let me go."

And he said, "No – but stay; what is that – in your breast?"

She was silent.

He said, "Open it, and let me see."

And she opened it. And against her breast was a tiny thing, who drank from it, and the yellow curls above his forehead pressed against it; and his knees were drawn up to her, and he held her breast fast with his hands.

And Reason said, "Who is he, and what is he doing here?"

And she said, "See his little wings – "

And Reason said, "Put him down."

And she said, "He is asleep, and he is drinking! I will carry him to the Land of Freedom. He has been a child so long, so long, I have carried him. In the Land of Freedom he will be a man. We will walk together there, and his great white wings will overshadow me. He has lisped one word only to me in the desert – 'Passion!' I have dreamed he might learn to say 'Friendship' in that land."

And Reason said, "Put him down!"

And she said, "I will carry him so – with one arm, and with the other I will fight the water."

He said, "Lay him down on the ground. When you are in the water you will forget to fight, you will think only of him. Lay him down." He said, "He will not die. When he finds you have left him alone he will open his wings and fly. He will be in the Land of Freedom before you. Those who reach the Land of Freedom, the first hand they see stretching down the bank to help them shall be Love's. He will be a man then, not a child. In your breast he cannot thrive; put him down that he may grow."

And she took her bosom from his mouth, and he bit her, so that the blood ran down on to the ground. And she laid him down on the earth; and she covered her wound. And she bent and stroked his wings. And I saw the hair on her forehead turned white as snow, and she had changed from youth to age.

And she stood far off on the bank of the river. And she said, "For what do I go to this far land which no one has ever reached? *Oh, I am alone! I am utterly alone!*"

And Reason, that old man, said to her, "Silence! What do you hear?"

And she listened intently, and she said, "I hear a sound of feet, a thousand times ten thousand and thousands of thousands, and they beat this way!"

He said, "They are the feet of those that shall follow you. Lead on! make a track to the water's edge! Where you stand now, the ground will be beaten flat by ten thousand times ten thousand feet." And he said, "Have you seen the locusts how they cross a stream? First one comes down to the water-edge, and it is swept away, and then another comes and then another, and then another, and at last with their bodies piled up a bridge is built and the rest pass over."

She said, "And, of those that come first, some are swept away, and are heard of no more; their bodies do not even build the bridge?"

"And are swept away, and are heard of no more – and what of that?" he said.

"And what of that – " she said.

"They make a track to the water's edge."

"They make a track to the water's edge –." And she said, "Over that bridge which shall be built with our bodies, who will pass?"

He said, "*The entire human race.*"

And the woman grasped her staff.

And I saw her turn down that dark path to the river.

And I awoke; and all about me was the yellow afternoon light: the sinking sun lit up the fingers of the milk bushes; and my horse stood by me quietly feeding. And I turned on my side, and I watched the ants run by thousands in the red sand. I thought I would go on my way now – the afternoon was cooler. Then a drowsiness crept over me again, and I laid back my head and fell asleep.

And I dreamed a dream.

I dreamed I saw a land. And on the hills walked brave women and brave men, hand in hand. And they looked into each other's eyes, and they were not afraid.

And I saw the women also hold each other's hands.

And I said to him beside me, "What place is this?"

And he said, "This is heaven."

And I said, "Where is it?"

And he answered, "On earth."

And I said, "When shall these things be?"

And he answered, "IN THE FUTURE."

And I awoke, and all about me was the sunset light; and on the low hills the sun lay, and a delicious coolness had crept over everything; and the ants were going slowly home. And I walked towards my horse, who stood quietly feeding. Then the sun passed down behind the hills; but I knew that the next day he would arise again.

First published in *The Fortnightly Review* August 1887: 198–203, where it bore the subtitle 'Under a Mimosa tree'.

# VI
## A Dream of Wild Bees

A mother sat alone at an open window. Through it came the voices of the children as they played under the acacia-trees, and the breath of the hot afternoon air. In and out of the room flew the bees, the wild bees, with their legs yellow with pollen, going to and from the acacia-trees, droning all the while. She sat on a low chair before the table and darned. She took her work from the great basket that stood before her on the table: some lay on her knee and half covered the book that rested there. She watched the needle go in and out; and the dreary hum of the bees and the noise of the children's voices became a confused murmur in her ears, as she worked slowly and more slowly. Then the bees, the long-legged wasp-like fellows who make no honey, flew closer and closer to her head, droning. Then she grew more and more drowsy, and she laid her hand, with the stocking over it, on the edge of the table, and leaned her head upon it. And the voices of the children outside grew more and more dreamy, came now far, now near; then she did not hear them, but she felt under her heart where the ninth child lay. Bent forward and sleeping there, with the bees flying about her head, she had a weird brain-picture; she thought the bees lengthened and lengthened themselves out and became human creatures and moved round and round her. Then one came to her softly, saying, "Let me lay my hand upon thy side where the child sleeps. If I shall touch him he shall be as I."

She asked, "Who are you?"

And he said, "I am Health. Whom I touch will have always the red blood dancing in his veins; he will not know weariness nor pain; life will be a long laugh to him."

"No," said another, "let me touch; for I am Wealth. If I touch him material care shall not feed on him. He shall live on the blood and sinews of his fellow-men, if he will; and what his eye lusts for, his hand will have. He shall not know 'I want.'" And the child lay still like lead.

And another said, "Let me touch him: I am Fame. The man I touch, I lead to a high hill where all men may see him. When he dies he is not forgotten, his name rings down the centuries, each echoes it on to his fellows. Think – not to be forgotten through the ages!"

And the mother lay breathing steadily, but in the brain-picture they pressed closer to her.

"Let me touch the child," said one, "for I am Love. If I touch him he shall not walk through life alone. In the greatest dark, when he puts out his hand he shall find another hand by it. When the world is against him, another shall say, '*You and I.*'" And the child trembled.

But another pressed close and said, "Let me touch; for I am Talent. I can do all things – that have been done before. I touch the soldier, the statesman, the thinker, and the politician who succeed; and the writer who is never before his time, and never behind it. If I touch the child he shall not weep for failure."

About the mother's head the bees were flying, touching her with their long tapering limbs; and, in her brain-picture, out of the shadow of the room came one with sallow face, deep-lined, the cheeks drawn into hollows, and a mouth smiling quiveringly. He stretched out his hand. And the mother drew back, and cried, "Who are you?" He answered nothing; and she looked up between his eyelids. And she said, "What can you give the child – health?" And he said, "The man I touch, there wakes up in his blood a burning fever, that shall lick his blood as fire. The fever that I will give him shall be cured when his life is cured."

"You give wealth?"

He shook his head. "The man whom I touch, when he bends to pick up gold, he sees suddenly a light over his head in the sky; while he looks up to see it, the gold slips from between his fingers, or sometimes another passing takes it from them."

"Fame?"

He answered, "Likely not. For the man I touch there is a path traced out in the sand by a finger which no man sees. That he must follow. Sometimes it leads almost to the top, and then turns down suddenly into the valley. He must follow it, though none else sees the tracing."

"Love?"

He said, "He shall hunger for it – but he shall not find it. When he stretches out his arms to it, and would lay his heart against a thing he loves, then, far off along the horizon he shall see a light play. He must go towards it. The thing he loves will not journey with him; he must travel alone. When he presses somewhat to his burning heart, crying, 'Mine, mine, my own!' he shall hear a voice – 'Renounce! renounce! this is not thine!'"

"He shall succeed?"

He said, "He shall fail. When he runs with others they shall reach the goal before him. For strange voices shall call to him and strange lights shall beckon him, and he must wait and listen. And this shall be the strangest: far off across the burning sands where, to other men, there is only the desert's waste, he shall see a blue sea! On that sea the sun shines always, and the water is blue as burning amethyst, and the foam is white on the shore. A great land rises from it, and he shall see upon the mountain-tops burning gold."

The mother said, "He shall reach it?"

And he smiled curiously.

She said, "It is real?"

And he said, "What *is* real?"

And she looked up between his half-closed eyelids, and said, "Touch."

And he leaned forward and laid his hand upon the sleeper, and whispered to it, smiling; and this only she heard – *"This shall be thy reward – that the ideal shall be real to thee."*

And the child trembled; but the mother slept on heavily and her brain-picture vanished. But deep within her the antenatal thing that lay here had a dream. In those eyes that had never seen the day, in that half-shaped brain was a sensation of light! Light – that it never had seen. Light – that perhaps it never should see. Light – that existed somewhere!

And already it had its reward: the Ideal was real to it.

*London.*

# VII
# In a Ruined Chapel

*"I cannot forgive – I love."*

There are four bare walls; there is a Christ upon the walls, in red, carrying his cross; there is a Blessèd Bambino with the face rubbed out; there is Madonna in blue and red; there are Roman soldiers and a Christ with tied hands. All the roof is gone; overhead is the blue, blue Italian sky; the rain has beaten holes in the walls, and the plaster is peeling from it. The chapel stands here alone upon the promontory, and by day and by night the sea breaks at its feet. Some say that it was set here by the monks from the island down below, that they might bring their sick here in times of deadly plague. Some say that it was set here that the passing monks and friars, as they hurried by upon the roadway, might stop and say their prayers here. Now no one stops to pray here, and the sick come no more to be healed.

Behind it runs the old Roman road. If you climb it and come and sit there alone on a hot sunny day you may almost hear at last the clink of the Roman soldiers upon the pavement, and the sound of that older time, as you sit there in the sun, when Hannibal and his men broke through the brushwood, and no road was.

Now it is very quiet. Sometimes a peasant girl comes riding by between her panniers, and you hear the mule's feet beat upon the bricks of the pavement; sometimes an old woman goes past with a bundle of weeds upon her head, or a brigand-looking man hurries by with a bundle of sticks in his hand; but for the rest the Chapel lies here alone upon the promontory, between the two bays and hears the sea break at its feet.

I came here one winter's day when the midday sun shone hot on the bricks of the Roman road. I was weary, and the way seemed steep. I walked into the chapel to the broken window, and looked out across the bay. Far off, across the blue, blue water, were towns and villages, hanging white and red dots, upon the mountain-sides, and the blue mountains rose up into the sky, and now stood out from it and now melted back again.

The mountains seemed calling to me, but I knew there would never be a bridge built from them to me; never, never, never! I shaded my eyes with my hand and turned away. I could not bear to look at them.

I walked through the ruined Chapel, and looked at the Christ in red carrying his cross, and the Blessèd rubbed-out Bambino, and the Roman soldiers, and the folded hands, and the reed; and I went and sat down in the open porch upon a stone. At my feet was the small bay, with its white row of houses buried among the olive trees; the water broke in a long, thin, white line of foam along the shore; and I leaned my elbows on my knees. I was tired, very tired; tired with a tiredness that seemed older than the heat of the day and the shining of the sun on the bricks of the Roman road; and I lay my head upon my knees; I heard the breaking of the water on the rocks three hundred feet below, and the rustling of the wind among the olive trees and the ruined arches, and then I fell asleep there. I had a dream.

A man cried up to God, and God sent down an angel to help him; and the angel came back and said, "I cannot help that man."

God said, "How is it with him?"

And the angel said, "He cries out continually that one has injured him; and he would forgive him and he cannot."

God said, "What have you done for him?"

The angel said, "All – . I took him by the hand, and I said, 'See, when other men speak ill of that man do you speak well of him; secretly, in ways he shall not know, serve him; if you have anything you value share it with him, so, serving him, you will at last come to feel possession in him, and you will forgive.' And he said, 'I will do it.' Afterwards, as I passed by in the dark of night, I heard one crying out, 'I have done all. It helps nothing! My speaking well of him helps me nothing! If I share my heart's blood with him, is the burning within me less? I cannot forgive; I cannot forgive! Oh, God, I cannot forgive!'

"I said to him, 'See here, look back on all your past. See from your childhood all smallness, all indirectness that has been yours; look well at it, and in its light do you not see every man your brother? Are you so sinless you have right to hate?'

"He looked, and said, 'Yes, you are right; I too have failed, and I forgive my fellow. Go, I am satisfied; I have forgiven;' and he laid him down peacefully and folded his hands on his breast, and I thought it was well with him. But scarcely had my wings rustled and I turned to come up here, when I heard one crying out on earth again, 'I cannot forgive! I cannot forgive! Oh, God, God, I cannot forgive! It is better to die than to hate! I cannot forgive! I cannot forgive!' And I went and stood outside his door in the dark, and I heard him cry, 'I have not sinned so, not so! If I have torn my fellows' flesh ever so little, I have kneeled down and kissed the wound with my mouth till it was healed. I have not willed that any soul shall be lost through hate of me. If they have but fancied that I wronged them I have lain down on the ground before them that they might tread on me, and so, seeing my humiliation, forgive and not be lost through hating me; they have not cared that my soul should be lost; they have not willed to save me; they have not tried that I should forgive them!'

"I said to him, 'See here, be thou content; do *not* forgive: forget this soul and its injury; go on your way. In the next world perhaps – '

"He cried, 'Go from me, you understand nothing! What is the next world to me! I am lost now, to-day. I cannot see the sunlight shine, the dust is in my throat, the sand is in my eyes! Go from me, you know nothing! Oh, once again before I die to see that the world is beautiful! Oh, God, God, I cannot live and not love. I cannot live and hate. Oh, God, God, God!' So I left him crying out and came back here."

God said, "This man's soul must be saved."

And the angel said "How?"

God said, "Go down you, and save it."

The angel said, "What more shall I do?"

Then God bent down and whispered in the angel's ear, and the angel spread out its wings and went down to earth.

And partly I woke, sitting there upon the broken stone with my head on my knee; but I was too weary to rise. I heard the wind roam through the olive trees and among the ruined arches, and then I slept again.

The angel went down and found the man with the bitter heart and took him by the hand, and led him to a certain spot.

Now the man wist not where it was the angel would take him nor what he would show him there. And when they came the angel shaded the man's eyes with his wing, and when he moved it the man saw somewhat on the earth before them. For God had given it to that angel to unclothe a human soul; to take from it all those outward attributes of form, and colour, and age, and sex, whereby one man is known from among his fellows and is marked off from the rest, and the soul lay before them, bare, as a man turning his eye inwards beholds himself.

They saw its past, its childhood, the tiny life with the dew upon it; they saw its youth when the dew was melting, and the creature raised its Lilliputian mouth to drink from a cup too large for it, and they saw how the water spilt; they saw its hopes that were never realized; they saw its hours of intellectual blindness, men call sin; they saw its hours of all-radiating insight, which men call righteousness; they saw its hour of strength, when it leaped to its feet crying, "I am omnipotent;" its hour of weakness, when it fell to the earth and grasped dust only; they saw what it might have been, but never would be.

The man bent forward.

And the angel said, "What is it?"

He answered, "It is *I*! It is myself!" And he went forward as if he would have lain his heart against it; but the angel held him back and covered his eyes.

Now God had given power to the angel further to unclothe that soul, to take from it all those outward attributes of time and place and circumstance whereby the individual life is marked off from the life of the whole.

Again the angel uncovered the man's eyes, and he looked. He saw before him that which in its tiny drop reflects the whole universe; he saw that which marks within itself the step of the furthest star, and tells how the crystal grows under ground where no eye has seen it; that which is where the germ in the egg stirs; which moves the outstretched fingers of the little newborn babe, and keeps the leaves of the trees pointing upward; which moves where the jelly-fish sail alone on the sunny seas, and is where the lichens form on the mountains' rocks.

And the man looked.

And the angel touched him.

But the man bowed his head and shuddered. He whispered – "*It is God!*"

And the angel re-covered the man's eyes. And when he uncovered them there was one walking from them a little way off; – for the angel had re-clothed the soul in its outward form and vesture – and the man knew who it was.

And the angel said, "Do you know him?"

And the man said, "I know him," and he looked after the figure.

And the angel said, "Have you forgiven him?"

But the man said, "*How beautiful my brother is!*"

And the angel looked into the man's eyes, and he shaded his own face with his wing from the light. He laughed softly and went up to God.

But the men were together on earth.

I awoke.

The blue, blue sky was over my head, and the waves were breaking below on the shore. I walked through the little chapel, and I saw the Madonna in blue and red, and the Christ carrying his cross, and the Roman soldiers with the rod, and the Blessèd Bambino with its broken face; and then I walked down the sloping rock to the brick pathway. The olive trees stood up on either side of the road, their black berries and pale-green leaves stood out against the sky; and the little ice-plants hung from the crevices in the stone wall. It seemed to me as if it must have rained while I was asleep. I thought I had never seen the heavens and the earth look so beautiful before. I walked down the road. The old, old, old tiredness was gone.

Presently there came a peasant boy down the path leading his ass; she had two large panniers fastened to her sides; and they went down the road before me.

I had never seen him before; but I should have liked to walk by him and to have held his hand – only, he would not have known why.

*Alassio, Italy.*

## VIII
## Life's Gifts

I saw a woman sleeping. In her sleep she dreamt Life stood before her, and held in each hand a gift – in the one Love, in the other Freedom. And she said to the woman, "Choose!"

And the woman waited long: and she said, "Freedom!"

And Life said, "Thou hast well chosen. If thou hadst said, 'Love,' I would have given thee that thou didst ask for; and I would have gone from thee, and returned to thee no more. Now, the day will come when I shall return. In that day I shall bear both gifts in one hand."

I heard the woman laugh in her sleep.

*London.*

# IX
# The Artist's Secret

There was an artist once, and he painted a picture. Other artists had colours richer and rarer, and painted more notable pictures. He painted his with one colour, there was a wonderful red glow on it; and the people went up and down, saying, "We like the picture, we like the glow."

The other artists came and said, "Where does he get his colour from?" They asked him; and he smiled and said, "I cannot tell you"; and worked on with his head bent low.

And one went to the far East and bought costly pigments, and made a rare colour and painted, but after a time the picture faded. Another read in the old books, and made a colour rich and rare, but when he had put it on the picture it was dead.

But the artist painted on. Always the work got redder and redder, and the artist grew whiter and whiter. At last one day they found him dead before his picture, and they took him up to bury him. The other men looked about in all the pots and crucibles, but they found nothing they had not.

And when they undressed him to put his grave-clothes on him, they found above his left breast the mark of a wound – it was an old, old wound, that must have been there all his life, for the edges were old and hardened; but Death, who seals all things, had drawn the edges together, and closed it up.

And they buried him. And still the people went about saying, "Where did he find his colour from?"

And it came to pass that after a while the artist was forgotten – but the work lived.

*St. Leonards-on-Sea.*

# X
# "I Thought I Stood"

I thought I stood in Heaven before God's throne, and God asked me what I had come for. I said I had come to arraign my brother, Man.

God said, "What has he done?"

I said, "He has taken my sister, Woman, and has stricken her, and wounded her, and thrust her out into the streets; she lies there prostrate. His hands are red with blood. *I* am here to arraign him; that the kingdom be taken from him, because he is not worthy, and given unto me. My hands are pure."

I showed them.

God said, "Thy hands are pure. – Lift up thy robe."

I raised it; my feet were red, blood-red, as if I had trodden in wine.

God said, "How is this?"

I said, "Dear Lord, the streets on earth are full of mire. If I should walk straight on in them my outer robe might be bespotted, you see how white it is! Therefore I pick my way."

God said, "*On what?*"

I was silent, and I let my robe fall. I wrapped my mantle about my head. I went out softly. I was afraid that the angels would see me.

## II

Once more I stood at the gate of Heaven, I and another. We held fast by one another; we were very tired. We looked up at the great gates; the angels opened them, and we went in. The mud was on our garments. We walked across the marble floor, and up to the great throne. Then the angels divided us. Her, they set upon the top step, but me, upon the bottom; for, they said, "Last time this woman came here she left red foot-marks on the floor; we had to wash them out with our tears. Let her not go up."

Then she, with whom I came, looked back, and stretched out her hand to me; and I went and stood beside her. And the angels, they, the shining ones who never sinned and never suffered, walked by us to and fro and up and down; I think we should have felt a little lonely there if it had not been for one another, the angels were so bright.

God asked me what I had come for; and I drew my sister forward a little that he might see her.

God said, "How is it you are here together to-day?"

I said, "She was upon the ground in the street, and they passed over her; I lay down by her, and she put her arms around my neck, and so I lifted her, and we two rose together."

God said, "Whom are you now come to accuse before me?"

I said, "We are come to accuse no man."

And God bent, and said, "My children – what is it that ye seek?"

And she beside me drew my hand that I should speak for both.

I said, "We have come to ask that thou shouldst speak to Man, our brother, and give us a message for him that he might understand, and that he might – "

God said, "Go, take the message down to him!"

I said, "But what *is* the message?"

God said, "Upon your hearts it is written; take it down to him."

And we turned to go; the angels went with us to the door. They looked at us.

And one said – "Ai! but their dresses are beautiful!"

And the other said, "I thought it was mire when they came in, but see, it is all golden!"

But another said, "Hush, it is the light from their faces!"

And we went down to him.

*Alassio, Italy.*

# XI
## The Sunlight Lay Across My Bed

In the dark one night I lay upon my bed. I heard the policeman's feet beat on the pavement; I heard the wheels of carriages roll home from houses of entertainment; I heard a woman's laugh below my window – and then I fell asleep. And in the dark I dreamt a dream. I dreamt God took my soul to Hell.

Hell was a fair place; the water of the lake was blue.
    I said to God, "I like this place."
    God said, "Ay, dost thou!"
    Birds sang, turf came to the water-edge, and trees grew from it. Away off among the trees I saw beautiful women walking. Their clothes were of many delicate colours and clung to them, and they were tall and graceful and had yellow hair. Their robes trailed over the grass. They glided in and out among the trees, and over their heads hung yellow fruit like large pears of melted gold.
    I said, "It is very fair; I would go up and taste the – "
    God said, "Wait."
    And after a while I noticed a very fair woman pass: she looked this way and that, and drew down a branch, and it seemed she kissed the fruit upon it softly, and went on her way, and her dress made no rustle as she passed over the grass. And when I saw her no more, from among the stems came another woman fair as she had been, in a delicate tinted robe; she looked this way and that. When she saw no one there she drew down the fruit, and when she had looked over it to find a place, she put her mouth to it softly, and went away. And I saw other and other women come, making no noise, and they glided away also over the grass.
    And I said to God, "What are they doing?"
    God said, "They are poisoning."
    And I said, "How?"
    God said, "They touch it with their lips, when they have made a tiny wound in it with their fore-teeth they set in it that which is under their tongues: they close it with their lip – that no man may see the place, – and pass on."
    I said to God, "Why do they do it?"

God said, "That another may not eat."

I said to God, "But if they poison all then none dare eat; what do they gain?"

God said, "Nothing."

I said, "Are they not afraid they themselves may bite where another has bitten?"

God said, "They are afraid. In Hell all men fear."

He called me further. And the water of the lake seemed less blue.

Then, to the right among the trees were men working. And I said to God, "I should like to go and work with them. Hell must be a very fruitful place, the grass is so green."

God said, "Nothing grows in the garden they are making."

We stood looking; and I saw them working among the bushes, digging holes, but in them they set nothing; and when they had covered them with sticks and earth each went a way off and sat behind the bushes watching; and I noticed that as each walked he set his foot down carefully looking where he trod. I said to God, "What are they doing?"

God said, "Making pitfalls into which their fellows may sink."

I said to God, "Why do they do it?"

God said, "Because each thinks that when his brother falls he will rise."

I said to God, "How will he rise?"

God said, "He will not rise."

And I saw their eyes gleam from behind the bushes.

I said to God, "Are these men sane?"

God said, "They are not sane; there is no sane man in Hell."

And he told me to come further.

And I looked where I trod.

And we came where Hell opened into a plain, and a great house stood there. Marble pillars upheld the roof, and white marble steps let up to it. The wind of heaven blew through it. Only at the back hung a thick curtain. Fair men and women there feasted at long tables. They danced, and I saw the robes of women flutter in the air and heard the laugh of strong men. What they feasted with was wine; they drew it from large jars which stood somewhat in the background, and I saw the wine sparkle as they drew it.

And I said to God, "I should like to go up and drink." And God said, "Wait." And I saw men coming in to the Banquet House; they came in from the back and lifted the corner of the curtain at the sides and crept in quickly; and they let the curtain fall behind them; they bore great jars they could hardly carry. And the men and women crowded round them, and the new-comers opened their jars and gave them of the wine to drink; and I saw that the women drank even more greedily than the men. And when others had well drunken they set the jars among the old ones beside the wall, and took their places at the table. And I saw that some of the jars were very old and mildewed and dusty, but others had still drops of new must on them and shone from the furnace.

And I said to God, "What is that?" For amid the sound of the singing, and over the dancing of feet, and over the laughing across the wine-cups I heard a cry.

And God said, "Stand a way off."

And he took me where I saw both sides of the curtain. Behind the house was the wine-press where the wine was made. I saw the grapes crushed, and I heard them cry. I said, "Do not they on the other side hear it?"

God said, "The curtain is thick; they are feasting."

And I said, "But the men who came in last. They saw?"

God said, "They let the curtain fall behind them – and they forget!"

I said, "How came they by their jars of wine?"

God said, "In the treading of the press these are they who came to the top; they have climbed out over the edge, and filled their jars from below, and have gone into the house."

And I said, "And if they had fallen as they climbed – ?"

God said, "They had been wine."

I stood a way off watching in the sunshine, and I shivered.

God lay in the sunshine watching too.

Then there rose one among the feasters, who said, "My brethren, let us pray!"

And all the men and women rose: and strong men bowed their heads, and mothers folded their little children's hands together, and turned their faces upwards, to the roof. And he who first had risen stood at the table head, and stretched out both his hands, and his beard was long and white, and his sleeves and his beard had been dipped in wine; and because the sleeves were wide and full they held much wine, and it dropped down upon the floor.

And he cried, "My brothers and my sisters, let us pray."

And all the men and women answered, "Let us pray."

He cried, "For this fair banquet-house we thank thee, Lord."

And all the men and women said "We thank thee, Lord."

"Thine is this house, dear Lord."

"Thine is this house."

"For us hast thou made it."

"For us."

"Oh, fill our jars with wine, dear Lord."

"Our jars with wine."

"Give peace and plenty in our time, dear Lord."

"Peace and plenty in our time" – I said to God, "Whom is it they are talking to?" God said, "Do *I* know whom they speak of?" And I saw they were looking up at the roof; but out in the sunshine, God lay.

" – dear Lord!"

"Dear Lord."

"Our children's children, Lord, shall rise and call thee blessed."

"Our children's children, Lord." – I said to God, "The grapes are crying!" God said, "Still! *I* hear them" – "shall call thee blessed."

"Shall call thee blessed."
"Pour forth more wine upon us, Lord."
"More wine."
"More wine."
"More wine!"
"Wine!!"
"Wine!!"
"Wine!!!"
"Dear Lord!"

Then men and women sat down and the feast went on. And mothers poured out wine and fed their little children with it, and men held up the cup to women's lips and cried, "Beloved! drink," and women filled their lovers' flagons and held them up; and yet the feast went on.

And after a while I looked, and I saw the curtain that hung behind the house moving.

I said to God, "Is it a wind?"

God said, "A wind."

And it seemed to me, that against the curtain I saw pressed the forms of men and women. And after a while the feasters saw it move, and they whispered, one to another. Then some rose and gathered the most worn-out cups, and into them they put what was left at the bottom of other vessels. Mothers whispered to their children, "Do not drink all, save a little drop when you have drunk." And when they had collected all the dregs they slipped the cups out under the bottom of the curtain without lifting it. After a while the curtain left off moving.

I said to God, "How is it so quiet?"

He said, "They have gone away to drink it."

I said, "*They* drink it – *their own*!"

God said, "It comes from this side of the curtain, and they are very thirsty."

Then the feast went on, and after a while I saw a small, white hand slipped in below the curtain's edge along the floor; and it motioned towards the wine jars.

And I said to God, "Why is that hand so bloodless?"

And God said, "It is a wine-pressed hand."

And men saw it and started to their feet; and women cried, and ran to the great wine jars, and threw their arms around them, and cried, "Ours, our own, our beloved!" and twined their long hair about them.

I said to God, "Why are they frightened of that one small hand?"

God answered, "Because it is so white."

And men ran in a great company towards the curtain, and struggled there. I heard them strike upon the floor. And when they moved away the curtain hung smooth and still; and there was a small stain upon the floor.

I said to God, "Why do they not wash it out?"

God said, "They cannot."

And they took small stones and put them down along the edge of the curtain to keep it down. Then the men and women sat down again at the tables.

And I said to God, "Will those stones keep it down?"

God said, "What think you?"

I said, "If the wind blew?–"

God said, "If the wind blew?"

And the feast went on.

And suddenly I cried to God, "If one should rise among them, even of themselves, and start up from the table and should cast away his cup, and cry, 'My brothers and my sisters, stay! what is it that we drink?' – and with his sword should cut in two the curtain, and holding wide the fragments, cry, 'Brothers, sisters, see! it is not wine, not wine! not wine! My brothers, oh, my sisters!' and he should overturn the – "

God said, "Be still! – , see there."

I looked: before the banquet-house, among the grass, I saw a row of mounds, flowers covered them, and gilded marble stood at their heads. I asked God what they were.

He answered, "They are the graves of those who rose up at the feast and cried."

And I asked God how they came there.

He said, "The men of the banquet-house rose and cast them down backwards."

I said, "Who buried them?"

God said, "The men who cast them down."

I said, "How came it that they threw them down, and then set marble over them?"

God said, "Because the bones cried out, they covered them."

And among the grass and weeds I saw an unburied body lying; and I asked God why it was.

God said, "Because it was thrown down only yesterday. In a little while, when the flesh shall have fallen from its bones, they will bury it also, and plant flowers over it."

And still the feast went on.

Men and women sat at the tables quaffing great bowls. Some rose, and threw their arms about each other, and danced and sang. They pledged each other in the wine, and kissed each other's blood-red lips.

Higher and higher grew the revels.

Men, when they had drunk till they could no longer, threw what was left in their glasses up to the roof, and let it fall back in cascades. Women dyed their children's garments in the wine, and fed them on it till their tiny mouths were red. Sometimes, as the dancers whirled, they overturned a vessel, and their garments were bespattered. Children sat upon the floor with great bowls of wine, and swam rose-leaves on it, for boats. They put their hands in the wine and blew large red bubbles.

And higher and higher grew the revels, and wilder the dancing, and louder and louder the singing. But here and there among the revellers were those who did not revel. I saw that at the tables here and there were men who sat with their elbows on the board and hands shading their eyes; they looked into the wine-cup beneath them, and did not drink. And when one touched them lightly on the shoulder, bidding them to rise and dance and sing, they started, and then looked down, and sat there watching the wine in the cup, but they did not move.

And here and there I saw a woman sit apart. The others danced and sang and fed their children, but she sat silent with her head aside as though she listened. Her little children plucked her gown; she did not see them; she was listening to some sound, but she did not stir.

The revels grew higher. Men drank till they could drink no longer, and lay their heads upon the table sleeping heavily. Women who could dance no more leaned back on the benches with their heads against their lovers' shoulders. Little children, sick with wine, lay down upon the edges of their mothers' robes. Sometimes, a man rose suddenly, and as he staggered struck the tables and overthrew the benches; some leaned upon the balustrades sick unto death. Here and there one rose who staggered to the wine jars and lay down beside them. He turned the wine tap, but sleep overcame him as he lay there, and the wine ran out.

Slowly the thin, red stream ran across the white marbled floor; it reached the stone steps; slowly, slowly, slowly it trickled down, from step to step, from step to step: then it sank into the earth. A thin white smoke rose up from it.

I was silent; I could not breathe; but God called me to come further.

And after I had travelled for a while I came where on seven hills lay the ruins of a mighty banquet-house larger and stronger than the one which I had seen standing.

I said to God, "What did the men who built it here?"

God said, "They feasted."

I said, "On what?"

God said, "On wine."

And I looked; and it seemed to me that behind the ruins lay still a large circular hollow within the earth where a foot of the wine-press had stood.

I said to God, "How came it that this large house fell?"

God said, "Because the earth was sodden."

He called me to come further.

And at last we came upon a hill where blue waters played, and white marble lay upon the earth. I said to God, "What was here once?"

God said, "A pleasure house."

I looked, and at my feet great pillars lay. I cried aloud for joy to God, "The marble blossoms!"

God said, "Ay, 'twas a fairy house. There has not been one like to it, nor ever shall be. The pillars and the porticoes blossomed; and the wine cups were as gathered flowers: on this side all the curtain was broidered with fair designs, the stitching was of gold."

I said to God, "How came it that it fell?"

God said, "On the side of the wine-press it was dark."

And as we travelled, we came where lay a mighty ridge of sand, and a dark river ran there; and there rose two vast mounds.

I said to God, "They are very mighty."

God said, "Ay, exceeding great."

And I listened.

God asked me what I was listening to.

And I said, "A sound of weeping, and I hear the sound of strokes, but I cannot tell whence it comes."

God said, "It is the echo of the wine-press lingering still among the coping-stones upon the mounds. A banquet-house stood here."

And he called me to come further.

Upon a barren hill-side, where the soil was arid, God called me to stand still. And I looked around.

God said, "There was a feasting-house here once upon a time."

I said to God, "I see no mark of any!"

God said, "There was not left one stone upon another that has not been thrown down." And I looked round; and on the hill-side was a lonely grave.

I said to God, "What lies there?"

He said, "A vine truss, bruised in the wine-press!"

And at the head of the grave stood a cross, and on its foot lay a crown of thorns.

And as I turned to go, I looked backward. The wine-press and the banquet-house were gone; but the grave yet stood.

And when I came to the edge of a long ridge there opened out before me a wide plain of sand. And when I looked downward I saw great stones lie shattered; and the desert sand had half covered them over.

I said to God, "There is writing on them, but I cannot read it."

And God blew aside the desert sand, and I read the writing: "Weighed in the balance, and found – " but the last word was wanting.

And I said to God, "It was a banquet-house?"

God said, "Ay, a banquet-house."

I said, "There was a wine-press here?"

God said, "There was a wine-press."

I asked no further question. I was very weary; I shaded my eyes with my hand, and looked through the pink evening light.

Far off, across the sand, I saw two figures standing. With wings upfolded high above their heads, and stern faces set, neither man nor beast, they looked out across the desert sand, watching, watching, watching! I did not ask God what they were, for I knew what the answer would be.

And, further and yet further, in the evening light, I looked with my shaded eyes.

Far off, where the sands were thick and heavy, I saw a solitary pillar standing: the crown had fallen, and the sand had buried it. On the broken pillar sat a grey owl-of-the-desert, with folded wings; and in the evening light I saw the desert fox creep past it, trailing his brush across the sand.

Further, yet further, as I looked across the desert, I saw the sand gathered into heaps as though it covered something.

I cried to God, "Oh, I am so weary."

God said, "You have seen only one half of Hell."

I said, "I cannot see more, I am afraid of Hell. In my own narrow little path I dare not walk because I think that one has dug a pitfall for me; and if I put my hand to take a fruit I draw it back again because I think it has been kissed already. If I look out across the plains, the mounds are burial heaps; and when I pass among the stones I hear them crying aloud. When I see men dancing I hear the time beaten in with sobs; and their wine is living! Oh, I cannot bear Hell!"

God said, "Where will you go?"

I said "To the earth from which I came; it was better there."

And God laughed at me; and I wondered why he laughed.

God said, "Come, and I will show you Heaven."

\*      \*      \*      \*      \*      \*

And partly I awoke. It was still and dark; the sound of the carriages had died in the street; the woman who laughed was gone; and the policeman's tread was heard no more. In the dark it seemed as if a great hand lay upon my heart, and crushed it. I tried to breathe and tossed from side to side; and then again I fell asleep, and dreamed.

God took me to the edge of that world. It ended. I looked down. The gulf, it seemed to me, was fathomless, and then I saw two bridges crossing it that both sloped upwards.

I said to God, "Is there no other way by which men cross it?"

God said, "One; it rises far from here and slopes straight upwards."

I asked God what the bridges' names were.

God said, "What matter for the names? Call them the Good, the True, the Beautiful, if you will – you will yet not understand them."

I asked God how it was I could not see the third.

God said, "It is seen only by those who climb it."

I said, "Do they all lead to one heaven?"

God said, "All Heaven is one: nevertheless some parts are higher than others; those who reach the higher may always go down to rest in the lower; but those in the lower may not have strength to climb to the higher; nevertheless the light is all one."

And I saw over the bridge nearest me, which was wider than the other, countless footmarks go. I asked God why so many went over it.

God said, "It slopes less deeply, and leads to the first heaven."

And I saw that some of the footmarks were of feet returning. I asked God how it was.

He said, "No man who has once entered Heaven ever leaves it; but some, when they have gone half way, turn back, because they are afraid there is no land beyond."

I said, "Has none ever returned?"

God said, "No; once in Heaven always in Heaven."

And God took me over. And when we came to one of the great doors – for Heaven has more doors than one, and they are all open – the posts rose up so high on either side I could not see the top, nor indeed if there were any.

And it seemed to me so wide that all Hell could go in through it.

I said to God, "Which is the larger, Heaven or Hell?"

God said, "Hell is as wide, but Heaven is deeper. All Hell could be engulfed in Heaven, but all Heaven could not be engulfed in Hell."

And we entered. It was a still great land. The mountains rose on every hand, and there was a pale clear light; and I saw it came from the rocks and stones. I asked God how it was.

But God did not answer me.

I looked and wondered, for I had thought Heaven would be otherwise. And after a while it began to grow brighter, as if the day were breaking, and I asked God if the sun were not going to rise.

God said, "No; we are coming to where the people are."

And as we went on it grew brighter and brighter till it was burning day; and on the rock were flowers blooming, and trees blossomed at the roadside; and streams of water ran everywhere, and I heard the birds singing; I asked God where they were.

God said, "It is the people calling to one another."

And when we came nearer I saw them walking, and they shone as they walked. I asked God how it was they wore no covering.

God said, "Because all their body gives the light; they dare not cover any part."

And I asked God what they were doing.

God said, "Shining on the plants that they may grow."

And I saw that some were working in companies, and some alone, but most were in twos, sometimes two men and sometimes two women; but generally there was one man and one woman; and I asked God how it was.

God said, "When one man and one woman shine together, it makes the most perfect light. Many plants need that for their growing. Nevertheless, there are more kinds of plants in Heaven than one, and they need many kinds of light."

And one from among the people came running towards me; and when he came near it seemed to me that he and I had played together when we were little children, and that we had been born on the same day. And I told God what I felt; God said, "All men feel so in Heaven when another comes towards them."

And he who ran towards me held my hand, and led me through the bright lights. And when we came among the trees he sang aloud, and his companion answered, and it was a woman, and he showed me to her. She said, "He must have water"; and she took some in her hands, and fed me (I had been afraid to drink of the water in Hell), and they gathered fruit for me, and gave it me to eat. They said, "We shone long to make it ripen," and they laughed together as they saw me eat it.

The man said, "He is very weary; he must sleep" (for I had not dared to sleep in Hell), and he laid my head on his companion's knee and spread her hair out over me. I slept, and all the while in my sleep I thought I heard the birds calling across me. And when I woke it was like early morning, with the dew on everything.

And the man took my hand and led me to a hidden spot among the rocks. The ground was very hard, but out of it were sprouting tiny plants, and there was a little stream running. He said, "This is a garden we are making, no one else knows of it. We shine here every day; see, the ground has cracked with our shining, and this little stream is bursting out. See, the flowers are growing."

And he climbed on the rocks and picked from above two little flowers with dew on them, and gave them to me. And I took one in each hand; my hands shone as I held them. He said, "This garden is for all when it is finished." And he went away to his companion, and I went out into the great pathway.

And as I walked in the light I heard a loud sound of much singing. And when I came nearer I saw one with closed eyes, singing, and his fellows were standing round him; and the light on the closed eyes was brighter than anything I had seen in Heaven. I asked one who it was. And he said, "Hush! Our singing bird."

And I asked why the eyes shone so.

And he said, "They cannot see, and we have kissed them till they shone so."

And the people gathered closer round him.

And when I went a little further I saw a crowd crossing among the trees of light with great laughter. When they came close I saw they carried one without hands or feet. And a light came from the maimed limbs so bright that I could not look at them.

And I said to one, "What is it?"

He answered, "This is our brother who once fell and lost his hands and feet, and since then he cannot help himself; but we have touched the maimed stumps so often that now they shine brighter than anything in Heaven. We pass him on that he may shine on things that need much heat. No one is allowed to keep him long, he belongs to all"; and they went on among the trees.

I said to God, "This is a strange land. I had thought blindness and maimedness were great evils. Here men make them to a rejoicing."

God said, "Didst thou then think that love had *need* of eyes and hands!"

And I walked down the shining way with palms on either hand. I said to God, "Ever since I was a little child and sat alone and cried, I have dreamed of this land, and now I will not go away again. I will stay here and shine." And I began to take off my garments, that I might shine as others in that land; but when I looked down I saw my body gave no light. I said to God, "How is it?"

God said, "Is there no dark blood in your heart; is it bitter against none?"

And I said, "Yes – "; and I thought – "Now is the time when I will tell God, that which I have been meaning to tell him all along, how badly my fellow-men have treated me. How they have misunderstood me. How I have intended to be magnanimous and generous to them, and they – ." And I began to tell God; but when I looked down all the flowers were withering under my breath, and I was silent.

And God called me to come up higher, and I gathered my mantle about me and followed him.

And the rocks grew higher and steeper on every side; and we came at last to a place where a great mountain rose, whose top was lost in the clouds. And on its side I saw men working; and they picked at the earth with huge picks; and I saw that they laboured mightily. And some laboured in companies, but most laboured singly. And I saw the drops of sweat fall from their foreheads, and the muscles of their arms stand out with labour. And I said, "I had not thought in heaven to see men labour so!" And I thought of the garden where men sang and loved, and I wondered that any should choose to labour on that bare mountain-side. And I saw upon the foreheads of the men as they worked a light, and the drops which fell from them as they worked had light.

And I asked God what they were seeking for.

And God touched my eyes, and I saw that what they found were small stones, which had been too bright for me to see before; and I saw that the light of the stones and the light on the men's foreheads was the same. And I saw that when one found a stone he passed it on to his fellow, and he to another, and he to another. No man kept the stone he found. And at times they gathered in great company about when a large stone was found, and raised a great shout so that the sky rang; then they worked on again.

And I asked God what they did with the stones they found at last. Then God touched my eyes again to make them stronger; and I looked, and at my very feet was a mighty crown. The light streamed out from it.

God said, "Each stone as they find it is set here."

And the crown was wrought according to a marvellous pattern; one pattern ran through all, yet each part was different.

I said to God, "How does each man know where to set his stone, so that the pattern is worked out?"

God said, "Because in the light his forehead sheds each man sees faintly outlined that full crown."

And I said, "But how is it that each stone is joined along its edges to its fellows, so that there is no seam anywhere?"

God said, "The stones are alive; they grow."

And I said, "But what does each man gain by his working?"

God said, "He sees his outline filled."

I said, "But those stones which are last set cover those which were first; and those will again be covered by those which come later."

God said, "They are covered, but not hid. The light is the light of all. Without the first, no last."

And I said to God, "When will this crown be ended?"

And God said, "Look up!"

I looked up; and I saw the mountain tower above me, but its summit I could not see; it was lost in the clouds.

God said no more.

And I looked at the crown: then a longing seized me. Like the passion of a mother for the child whom death has taken; like the yearning of a friend for the friend whom life has buried; like the hunger of dying eyes for a life that is slipping; like the thirst of a soul for love at its first spring waking, so, but fiercer was the longing in me.

I cried to God, "I too will work here; I too will set stones in the wonderful pattern; it shall grow beneath *my* hand. And if it be that, labouring here for years, I should not find one stone, at least I will be with the men that labour here. I shall hear their shout of joy when each stone is found; I shall join in their triumph, I shall shout among them; I shall see the crown grow." So great was my longing as I looked at the crown, I thought a faint light fell from my forehead also.

God said, "Do you not hear the singing in the gardens?"

I said, "No, I hear nothing; I see only the crown." And I was dumb with longing; I forgot all the flowers of the lower Heaven and the singing there. And I ran forward, and threw my mantle on the earth and bent to seize one of the mighty tools which lay there. I could not lift it from the earth.

God said, "Where hast *thou* earned the strength to raise it? Take up thy mantle."

And I took up my mantle and followed where God called me; but I looked back, and I saw the crown burning, my crown that I had loved.

Higher and higher we climbed, and the air grew thinner. Not a tree or plant was on the bare rocks, and the stillness was unbroken. My breath came hard and quick, and the blood crept within my finger-tips. I said to God, "Is this Heaven?"

God said, "Yes; it is the highest."

And still we climbed. I said to God, "I cannot breathe so high."

God said, "Because the air is pure?"

And my head grew dizzy, and as I climbed the blood burst from my finger-tips.

Then we came out upon a lonely mountain-top.

No living being moved there; but far off on a solitary peak I saw a lonely figure standing. Whether it were man or woman I could not tell; for partly it seemed the figure of a woman, but its limbs were the mighty limbs of a man. I asked God whether it was man or woman.

God said, "In the least Heaven sex reigns supreme; in the higher it is not noticed; but in the highest it does not exist."

And I saw the figure bend over its work, and labour mightily, but what it laboured at I could not see.

I said to God, "How came it here?"

God said, "By a bloody stair. Step by step it mounted from the lowest Hell, and day by day as Hell grew farther and Heaven no nearer, it hung alone between two worlds. Hour by hour in that bitter struggle its limbs grew larger, till there fell from it rag by rag the garments which it started with. Drops fell from its eyes as it strained them; each step it climbed was wet with blood. Then it came out here."

And I thought of the garden where men sang with their arms around one another; and the mountain-side where they worked in company. And I shuddered.

And I said, "Is it not terribly alone here?"

God said, "It is never alone!"

I said, "What has it for all its labour? I see nothing return to it."

Then God touched my eyes, and I saw stretched out beneath us the plains of Heaven and Hell, and all that was within them.

God said, "From that lone height on which he stands, all things are open. To him is clear the shining in the garden, he sees the flower break forth and the streams sparkle; no shout is raised upon the mountain-side but his ear may hear it. He sees the crown grow and the light shoot from it. All Hell is open to him. He sees the paths mount upwards. To him, Hell is the seed ground from which Heaven springs. He sees the sap ascending."

And I saw the figure bend over its work, and the light from its face fell upon it.

And I said to God, "What is it making?"

And God said, "Music!"

And he touched my ears, and I heard it.

And after a long while I whispered to God, "This is Heaven."

And God asked me why I was crying. But I could not answer for joy.

And the face turned from its work, and the light fell upon me. Then it grew so bright I could not see things separately; and which were God, or the man, or I, I could not tell; we were all blended. I cried to God, "Where are you?" but there was no answer, only music and light.

Afterwards, when it had grown so dark again that I could see things separately, I found that I was standing there wrapped tight in my little old, brown, earthly cloak, and God and the man were separated from each other, and from me.

I did not dare say I would go and make music beside the man. I knew I could not reach even to his knee, nor move the instrument he played. But I thought I would stand there on my little peak and sing an accompaniment to that great music. And I tried; but my voice failed. It piped and quavered. I could not sing that tune. I was silent.

Then God pointed to me, that I should go out of Heaven.

And I cried to God, "Oh, let me stay here! If indeed it be, as I know it is, that I am not great enough to sing upon the mountain, nor strong enough to labour on its side, nor bright enough to shine and love within the garden, at least let me go down to the great gateway; humbly I will kneel there sweeping; and, as the saved pass in, I will see the light upon their faces. I shall hear the singing in the garden, and the shout upon the hillside – "

God said, "It may not be;" he pointed.

And I cried, "If I may not stay in Heaven, then let me go down to Hell, and I will grasp the hands of men and women there; and slowly, holding one another's hands, we will work our way upwards."

Still God pointed.

And I threw myself upon the earth and cried, "Earth is so small, so mean! It is not meet a soul should see Heaven and be cast out again!"

And God laid his hand on me, and said, "Go back to earth: *that which you seek is there.*"

I awoke: it was morning. The silence and darkness of the night were gone. Through my narrow attic window I saw the light of another day. I closed my eyes and turned towards the wall: I could not look upon the dull grey world.

In the streets below, men and women streamed past by hundreds; I heard the beat of their feet on the pavement. Men on their way to business; servants on errands; boys hurrying to school; weary professors pacing slowly the old street; prostitutes, men and women, dragging their feet wearily after last night's debauch; artists with quick, impatient footsteps; tradesmen for orders; children to seek for bread. I heard the stream beat by. And at the alley's mouth, at the street corner, a broken barrel-organ was playing; sometimes it quavered and almost stopped, then went on again, like a broken human voice.

I listened: my heart scarcely moved; it was as cold as lead. I could not bear the long day before me; and I tried to sleep again; yet still I heard the feet upon the pavement. And suddenly I heard them cry loud as they beat, "We are seeking! – we are seeking! – we are seeking!" and the broken barrel-organ at the street corner sobbed, "The Beautiful! – the Beautiful! – the Beautiful!" And my heart, which had been dead, cried out with every throb, "Love! – Truth! – the Beautiful! – the Beautiful!" It was the music I had heard in Heaven that I could not sing there.

And fully I awoke.

Upon the faded quilt, across my bed a long yellow streak of pale London sunlight was lying. It fell through my narrow attic window.

I laughed. I rose.

I was glad the long day was before me.

*Paris and London.*

First published in *The New Review* April 1890: 300–309; May 1890: 423–31.

Ralph Iron

# Dream Life
# and Real Life

DEDICATION.

**To
MY BROTHER FRED,**
FOR WHOSE SCHOOL MAGAZINE THE
FIRST OF THESE LITTLE STORIES—
ONE OF THE FIRST I EVER
MADE—WAS WRITTEN OUT
MANY LONG YEARS
AGO.

R. I.

NEW COLLEGE, EASTBOURNE.
*Sept. 29th, 1893*

# I
# A Little African Story

Little Jannita sat alone beside a milk-bush. Before her and behind her stretched the plain, covered with red sand and thorny "Karroo" bushes; and here and there a milk-bush, looking like a bundle of pale green rods tied together. Not a tree was to be seen anywhere, except on the banks of the river, and that was far away, and the sun beat on her head. Round her fed the Angora goats she was herding; pretty things, especially the little ones, with white silky curls that touched the ground. But Jannita sat crying. If an angel should gather up in his cup all the tears that have been shed, I think the bitterest would be those of children.

By and by she was so tired, and the sun was so hot, she laid her head against the milk-bush, and dropped asleep.

She dreamed a beautiful dream. She thought that when she went back to the farmhouse in the evening, the walls were covered with vines and roses, and the "kraals" (*sheepfolds*) were not made of red stone, but of lilac trees full of blossom. And the fat old Boer smiled at her, and the stick he held across the door for the goats to jump over, was a lily rod with seven blossoms at the end. When she went to the house her mistress gave her a whole roaster-cake for her supper, and the mistress's daughter had stuck a rose in the cake; and her mistress's son-in-law said "Thank you!" when she pulled off his boots, and did not kick her.

It was a beautiful dream.

While she lay thus dreaming, one of the little kids came and licked her on her cheek, because of the salt from her dried-up tears. And in her dream she was not a poor indentured child any more, living with Boers. It was her father who kissed her. He said he had only been asleep — that day when he lay down under the thorn-bush; he had not really died. He felt her hair, and said it was grown long and silky, and he said they would go back to Denmark now. He asked her why her feet were bare, and what the marks on her back were. Then he put her head on his shoulder, and picked her up, and carried her away, away! She laughed — she could feel her face against his brown beard. His arms were so strong.

As she lay there dreaming with the ants running over her naked feet, and with her brown curls lying in the sand, a Hottentot came up to her. He was dressed in ragged yellow trousers, and a dirty shirt, and torn jacket. He had a red handkerchief round his head, and a felt hat above that. His nose was flat, his eyes like slits, and the wool on his head was gathered into little round balls. He came to the milk-bush, and looked at the little girl lying in the hot sun. Then he walked off, and caught one of the fattest little Angora goats, and held its mouth fast, as he stuck it under his arm. He looked back to see that she was still sleeping, and jumped down into one of the "sluits." (*The deep fissures, generally dry, in which the superfluous torrents of water are carried from the "Karroo" plains after thunderstorms.*) He walked down the bed of the "sluit" a little way and came to an overhanging bank, under which, sitting on the red sand, were two men. One was a tiny, ragged, old bushman, four feet high; the other was an English navvy, in a dark blue blouse. They cut the kid's throat with the navvy's long knife, and covered up the blood with sand, and buried the entrails and skin. Then they talked, and quarrelled a little; and then they talked quietly again.

The Hottentot man put a leg of the kid under his coat and left the rest of the meat for the two in the "sluit," and walked away.

When little Jannita awoke it was almost sunset. She sat up very frightened, but her goats were all about her. She began to drive them home. "I do not think there are any lost," she said.

Dirk, the Hottentot, had brought his flock home already, and stood at the "kraal" door with his ragged yellow trousers. The fat old Boer put his stick across the door, and let Jannita's goats jump over, one by one. He counted them. When the last jumped over: "Have you been to sleep to-day?" he said; "there is one missing."

Then little Jannita knew what was coming, and she said, in a low voice, "No." And then she felt in her heart that deadly sickness that you feel when you tell a lie; and again she said, "Yes."

"Do you think you will have any supper this evening?" said the Boer.

"No," said Jannita.

"What do you think you will have?"

"I don't know," said Jannita.

"Give me your whip," said the Boer to Dick, the Hottentot.

---

The moon was all but full that night. Oh, but its light was beautiful!

The little girl crept to the door of the outhouse where she slept, and looked at it. When you are hungry, and very, very sore, you do not cry. She leaned her chin on one hand, and looked, with her great dove's eyes — the other hand was cut open, so she wrapped it in her pinafore. She looked across the plain at the sand and the low karroo-bushes, with the moonlight on them.

Presently, there came slowly, from far away, a wild spring-buck. It came close to the house, and stood looking at it in wonder, while the moonlight glinted on its horns, and in its great eyes. It stood wondering at the red brick walls, and the girl watched it. Then, suddenly, as if it scorned it all, it curved its beautiful back and turned; and away it fled over the bushes and sand, like a sheeny streak of white lightning. She stood up to watch it. So free, so free! Away, away! She watched, till she could see it no more on the wide plain.

Her heart swelled, larger, larger, larger: she uttered a low cry; and without waiting, pausing, thinking, she followed on its track. Away, away, away! "I – I also!" she said, "I – I also!"

When at last her legs began to tremble under her, and she stopped to breathe, the house was a speck behind her. She dropped on the earth, and held her panting sides.

She began to think now.

If she stayed on the plain they would trace her footsteps in the morning and catch her; but if she waded in the water in the bed of the river they would not be able to find her footmarks; and she would hide, there where the rocks and the "kopjes" were.

*("Kopjes," in the karroo, are hillocks of stones, that rise up singly or in clusters, here and there; presenting sometimes the fantastic appearance of old ruined castles or giant graves, the work of human hands.)*

So she stood up and walked towards the river. The water in the river was low; just a line of silver in the broad bed of sand, here and there broadening into a pool. She stepped into it, and bathed her feet in the delicious cold water. Up and up the stream she walked, where it rattled over the pebbles, and past where the farmhouse lay; and where the rocks were large, she leaped from one to the other. The night wind in her face made her strong — she laughed. She had never felt such night wind before. So the night smells to the wild bucks, because they are free! A free thing feels as a chained thing never can.

At last she came to a place where the willows grew on each side of the river, and trailed their long branches on the sandy bed. She could not tell why, she could not tell the reason, but a feeling of fear came over her.

On the left bank rose a chain of "kopjes" and a precipice of rocks. Between the precipice and the river bank there was a narrow path covered by the fragments of fallen rock. And upon the summit of the precipice a kippersol tree grew, whose palm-like leaves were clearly cut out against the night sky. The rocks cast a deep shadow, and the willow trees, on either side of the river. She paused, looked up and about her, and then ran on, fearful.

"What was I afraid of? How foolish I have been!" she said, when she came to a place where the trees were not so close together. And she stood still and looked back and shivered.

At last her steps grew wearier and wearier. She was very sleepy now, she could scarcely lift her feet. She stepped out of the river-bed. She only saw that the rocks about her were wild, as though many little "kopjes" had been broken up and strewn upon the ground, lay down at the foot of an aloe, and fell asleep.

---

But, in the morning, she saw what a glorious place it was. The rocks were piled on one another, and tossed this way and that. Prickly pears grew among them, and there were no less than six kippersol trees scattered here and there among the broken "kopjes." In the rocks, there were hundreds of homes for the coneys, and from the crevices wild asparagus hung down. She ran to the river, bathed in the clear cold water, and tossed it over her head. She sang aloud. All the songs she knew were sad, so she could not sing them now, she was glad, she was so free; but she sang the notes without the words, as the cock-o-veets do. Singing and jumping all the way, she went back, and took a sharp stone, and cut at the root of a kippersol, and got out a large piece, as long as her arm, and sat to chew it. Two coneys came out on the rock above her head and peeped at her. She held them out a piece, but they did not want it, and ran away.

It was very delicious to her. Kippersol is like raw quince, when it is very green; but she liked it. When good food is thrown at you by other people, strange to say, it is very bitter; but whatever you find yourself is sweet!

When she had finished she dug out another piece, and went to look for a pantry to put it in. At the top of a heap of rocks up which she clambered she found that some large stones stood apart but met at the top, making a room.

"Oh, this is my little home!" she said.

At the top and all round it was closed, only in the front it was open. There was a beautiful shelf in the wall for the kippersol, and she scrambled down again. She brought a great branch of prickly pear, and stuck it in a crevice before the door, and hung wild asparagus over it, till it looked as though it grew there. No one could see that there was a room there, for she left only a tiny opening, and hung a branch of feathery asparagus over it. Then she crept in to see how it looked. There was a glorious soft green light. Then she went out and picked some of those purple little ground flowers – you know them – those that keep their faces close to the ground, but when you turn them up and look at them they are deep blue eyes looking into yours! She took them with a little earth, and put them in the crevices between the rocks; and so the room was quite furnished. Afterwards she went down to the river and brought her arms full of willow, and made a lovely bed; and, because the weather was very hot, she lay down to rest upon it.

She went to sleep soon, and slept long, for she was very weak. Late in the afternoon she was awakened by a few cold drops falling on her face. She sat up. A great and fierce thunderstorm had been raging, and a few of the cool drops had fallen through the crevice in the rocks. She pushed the asparagus branch aside, and looked out, with her little hands folded about her knees. She heard the thunder rolling, and saw the red torrents rush among the stones on their way to the river. She heard the roar of the river as it now rolled, angry and red, bearing away stumps and trees on its muddy water. She listened and smiled, and pressed closer to the rock that took care of her. She pressed the palm of her hand against it. When you have no one to love you, you love the dumb things very much. When the sun set, it cleared up. Then the little girl ate some kippersol, and lay down again to sleep. She thought there was nothing so nice as to sleep. When one has had no food but kippersol juice for two days, one doesn't feel strong.

"It is so nice here," she thought, as she went to sleep, "I will stay here always."

Afterwards the moon rose. The sky was very clear now, there was not a cloud anywhere; and the moon shone in through the bushes in the door, and made a lattice-work of light on her face. She was dreaming a beautiful dream. The loveliest dreams of all are dreamed when you are hungry. She thought she was walking in a beautiful place, holding her father's hand, and they both had crowns on their head, crowns of wild asparagus. The people whom they passed smiled and kissed her; some gave her flowers, and some gave her food, and the sunlight was everywhere. She dreamed the same dream over and over, and it grew more and more beautiful; till, suddenly, it seemed as though she were standing quite alone. She looked up: on one side of her was the high precipice, on the other was the river, with the willow trees, drooping their branches into the water; and the moonlight was over all. Up, against the night sky the pointed leaves of the kippersol trees were clearly marked, and the rocks and the willow trees cast dark shadows.

In her sleep she shivered, and half awoke.

"Ah, I am not there, I am here," she said; and she crept closer to the rock, and kissed it, and went to sleep again.

It must have been about three o'clock, for the moon had begun to sink towards the western sky, when she woke, with a violent start. She sat up, and pressed her hand against her heart.

"What can it be? A coney must surely have run across my feet and frightened me!" she said, and she turned to lie down again; but soon she sat up. Outside, there was the distinct sound of thorns crackling in a fire.

She crept to the door and made an opening in the branches with her fingers.

A large fire was blazing in the shadow, at the foot of the rocks. A little Bushman sat over some burning coals that had been raked from it, cooking meat. Stretched on the ground was an Englishman, dressed in a blouse, and with a heavy, sullen face. On the stone beside him was Dirk, the Hottentot, sharpening a bowie knife.

She held her breath. Not a coney in all the rocks was so still.

"They can never find me here," she said; and she knelt, and listened to every word they said. She could hear it all.

"You may have all the money," said the Bushman; "but I want the cask of brandy. I will set the roof alight in six places, for a Dutchman burnt my mother once alive in a hut, with three children."

"You are sure there is no one else on the farm?" said the navvy.

"No, I have told you till I am tired," said Dirk; "the two Kaffirs have gone with the son to town; and the maids have gone to a dance; there is only the old man and the two women left."

"But suppose," said the navvy, "he should have the gun at his bedside, and loaded!"

"He never has," said Dirk; "it hangs in the passage, and the cartridges too. He never thought when he bought it what work it was for! I only wish the little white girl was there still," said Dirk; "but she is drowned. We traced her footmarks to the great pool that has no bottom."

She listened to every word, and they talked on.

Afterwards, the little Bushman, who crouched over the fire, sat up suddenly, listening.

"Ha! what is that?" he said.

A Bushman is like a dog: his ear is so fine he knows a jackal's tread from a wild dog's.

"I heard nothing," said the navvy.

"I heard," said the Hottentot; "but it was only a coney on the rocks."

"No coney, no coney," said the Bushman; "see, what is that there moving in the shade round the point?"

"Nothing! you idiot," said the navvy. "Finish your meat; we must start now."

There were two roads to the homestead. One went along the open plain, and was by far the shortest; but you might be seen half a mile off. The other ran along the river bank, where there were rocks, and holes, and willow-trees to hide among. And all down the river bank ran a little figure.

The river was swollen by the storm full to its banks, and the willow-trees dipped their half-drowned branches into its water. Wherever there was a gap between them, you could see it flow, red and muddy, with the stumps upon it. But the little figure ran on and on; never looking, never thinking; panting, panting! There, where the rocks were the thickest; there, where on the open space the moonlight shone; there, where the prickly pears were tangled, and the rocks cast shadows, on it ran; the little hands clenched, the little heart beating, the eyes fixed always ahead.

It was not far to run now. Only the narrow path between the high rocks and the river.

At last she came to the end of it, and stood for an instant. Before her lay the plain, and the red farm-house, so near, that if persons had been walking there you might have seen them in the moonlight. She clasped her hands. "Yes, I will tell them, I will tell them!" she said; "I am almost there!" She ran forward again, then hesitated. She shaded her eyes from the moonlight, and looked. Between her and the farm-house there were three figures moving over the low bushes.

In the sheeny moonlight you could see how they moved on, slowly and furtively; the short one, and the one in light clothes, and the one in dark.

"I cannot help them now!" she cried, and sank down on the ground, with her little hands clasped before her.

---

"Awake, awake!" said the farmer's wife; "I hear a strange noise; something calling, calling, calling!"

The man rose, and went to the window.

"I hear it also," he said; "surely some jackal's at the sheep. I will load my gun and go and see."

"It sounds to me like the cry of no jackal," said the woman; and when he was gone she woke her daughter.

"Come, let us go and make a fire, I can sleep no more," she said; "I have heard a strange thing to-night. Your father said it was a jackal's cry, but no jackal cries so. It was a child's voice, and it cried, 'Master, master, wake!'"

The women looked at each other; then they went to the kitchen, and made a great fire; and they sang psalms all the while.

At last the man came back; and they asked him, "What have you seen?" "Nothing," he said, "but the sheep asleep in their kraals, and the moonlight on the walls. And yet, it did seem to me," he added, "that far away near the 'krantz' [precipice] by the river, I saw three figures moving. And afterwards – it might have been fancy – I thought I heard the cry again; but since that, all has been still there."

---

Next day a navvy had returned to the railway works.

"Where have you been so long?" his comrades asked.

"He keeps looking over his shoulder," said one, "as though he thought he should see something there."

"When he drank his grog to-day," said another, "he let it fall, and looked round."

Next day, a small old Bushman, and a Hottentot, in ragged yellow trousers, were at a wayside canteen. When the Bushman had had brandy, he began to tell how something (he did not say whether it was man, woman, or child) had lifted up its hands and cried for mercy; had kissed a white man's hands, and cried to him to help it. Then the Hottentot took the Bushman by the throat, and dragged him out.

Next night, the moon rose up, and mounted the quiet sky. She was full now, and looked in at the little home; at the purple flowers stuck about the room, and the kippersol on the shelf. Her light fell on the willow trees, and on the high rocks, and on a little new-made heap of earth and round stones. Three men knew what was under it; and no one else ever will.

*Lily Kloof,*
*South Africa.*

First published in *The New College Magazine* (Eastbourne) November 1881.

# II
# The Woman's Rose

I have an old, brown carved box; the lid is broken and tied with a string. In it I keep little squares of paper, with hair inside, and a little picture which hung over my brother's bed when we were children, and other things as small. I have in it a rose. Other women also have such boxes where they keep such trifles, but no one has my rose.

When my eye is dim, and my heart grows faint, and my faith in woman flickers, and her present is an agony to me, and her future a despair, the scent of that dead rose, withered for twelve years, comes back to me. I know there will be spring; as surely as the birds know it when they see above the snow two tiny, quivering green leaves. Spring cannot fail us.

There were other flowers in the box once; a bunch of white acacia flowers, gathered by the strong hand of a man, as we passed down a village street on a sultry afternoon, when it had rained, and the drops fell on us from the leaves of the acacia trees. The flowers were damp; they made mildew marks on the paper I folded them in. After many years I threw them away. There is nothing of them left in the box now, but a faint, strong smell of dried acacia, that recalls that sultry summer afternoon; but the rose is in the box still.

It is many years ago now; I was a girl of fifteen, and I went to visit in a small up-country town. It was young in those days, and two days' journey from the nearest village; the population consisted mainly of men. A few were married, and had their wives and children, but most were single. There was only one young girl there when I came. She was about seventeen, fair, and rather fully-fleshed; she had large dreamy blue eyes, and wavy light hair; full, rather heavy lips, until she smiled; then her face broke into dimples, and all her white teeth shone. The hotel-keeper may have had a daughter, and the farmer in the outskirts had two, but we never saw them. She reigned alone. All the men worshipped her. She was the only woman they had to think of. They talked of her on the "stoep", at the market, at the hotel; they watched for her at street corners; they hated the man she bowed to or walked with down the street. They brought flowers to the front door; they offered her their horses; they begged her to marry them when they dared. Partly, there was something noble and heroic in this devotion of men to the best woman they knew; partly there was something natural in it, that these men, shut off from the world, should pour at the feet of one woman the worship that otherwise would have been given to twenty; and partly there was something mean in their envy of one another. If she had raised her little finger, I suppose, she might have married any one out of twenty of them.

Then I came. I do not think I was prettier; I do not think I was so pretty as she was. I was certainly not as handsome. But I was vital, and I was new, and she was old—they all forsook her and followed me. They worshipped me. It was to my door that the flowers came; it was I had twenty horses offered me when I could only ride one; it was for me they waited at street corners; it was what I said and did that they talked of. Partly I liked it. I had lived alone all my life; no one ever had told me I was beautiful and a woman. I believed them. I did not know it was simply a fashion, which one man had set and the rest followed unreasoningly. I liked them to ask me to marry them, and to say, No. I despised them. The mother heart had not swelled in me yet; I did not know all men were my children, as the large woman knows when her heart is grown. I was too small to be tender. I liked my power. I was like a child with a new whip, which it goes about cracking everywhere, not caring against what. I could not wind it up and put it away. Men were curious creatures, who liked me, I could never tell why. Only one thing took from my pleasure; I could not bear that they had deserted her for me. I liked her great dreamy blue eyes, I liked her slow walk and drawl; when I saw her sitting among men, she seemed to me much too good to be among them; I would have given all their compliments if she would once have smiled at me as she smiled at them, with all her face breaking into radiance, with her dimples and flashing teeth. But I knew it never could be; I felt sure she hated me; that she wished I was dead; that she wished I had never come to the village. She did not know, when we went out riding, and a man who had always ridden beside her came to ride beside me, that I sent him away; that once when a man thought to win my favour by ridiculing her slow drawl before me, I turned on him so fiercely that he never dared come before me again. I knew she knew that at the hotel men had made a bet as to which was the prettier, she or I, and had asked each man who came in, and that the one who had staked on me won. I hated them for it, but I would not let her see that I cared about what she felt towards me.

She and I never spoke to each other.

If we met in the village street we bowed and passed on; when we shook hands we did so silently, and did not look at each other. But I thought she felt my presence in a room just as I felt hers.

At last the time for my going came. I was to leave the next day. Some one I knew gave a party in my honour, to which all the village was invited.

It was midwinter. There was nothing in the gardens but a few dahlias and chrysanthemums, and I suppose that for two hundred miles round there was not a rose to be bought for love or money. Only in the garden of a friend of mine, in a sunny corner between the oven and the brick wall, there was a rose tree growing which had on it one bud. It was white, and it had been promised to the fair haired girl to wear at the party.

The evening came; when I arrived and went to the waiting-room, to take off my mantle, I found the girl there already. She was dressed in pure white, with her great white arms and shoulders showing, and her bright hair glittering in the candle-light, and the white rose fastened at her breast. She looked like a queen. I said "Good evening," and turned away quickly to the glass to arrange my old black scarf across my old black dress.

Then I felt a hand touch my hair.

"Stand still," she said.

I looked in the glass. She had taken the white rose from her breast, and was fastening it in my hair.

"How nice dark hair is; it sets off flowers so." She stepped back and looked at me. "It looks much better there!"

I turned round.

"You are so beautiful to me," I said.

"Y-e-s," she said, with her slow Colonial drawl; "I'm so glad."

We stood looking at each other.

Then they came in and swept us away to dance. All the evening we did not come near to each other. Only once, as she passed, she smiled at me.

The next morning I left the town.

I never saw her again.

Years afterwards I heard she had married and gone to America; it may or may not be so—but the rose—the rose is in the box still! When my faith in woman grows dim, and it seems that for want of love and magnanimity she can play no part in any future heaven; then the scent of that small withered thing comes back:—spring cannot fail us.

*Matjesfontein,*
*South Africa.*

First published in *The New Review* June 1891; 540–43.

# III
# "The Policy In Favour of Protection—".

*Was it Right?—Was it Wrong?*

A woman sat at her desk in the corner of a room; behind her a fire burnt brightly.

Presently a servant came in and gave her a card.

"Say I am busy and can see no one now. I have to finish this article by two o'clock."

The servant came back. The caller said she would only keep her a moment: it was necessary she should see her.

The woman rose from her desk. "Tell the boy to wait. Ask the lady to come in."

A young woman in a silk dress, with a cloak reaching to her feet, entered. She was tall and slight, with fair hair.

"I knew you would not mind. I wished to see you so!"

The woman offered her a seat by the fire. "May I loosen your cloak?—the room is warm."

"I wanted so to come and see you. You are the only person in the world who could help me! I know you are so large, and generous, and kind to other women!" She sat down. Tears stood in her large blue eyes: she was pulling off her little gloves unconsciously.

"You know Mr.—" (she mentioned the name of a well-known writer): "I know you meet him often in your work. I want you to do something for me!"

The woman on the hearth-rug looked down at her.

"I couldn't tell my father or my mother, or any one else; but I can tell you, though I know so little of you. You know, last summer he came and stayed with us a month. I saw a great deal of him. I don't know if he liked me; I know he liked my singing, and we rode together—I liked him more than any man I have ever seen. Oh, you know it isn't true that a woman can only like a man when he likes her; and I thought, perhaps, he liked me a little. Since we have been in town we have asked, but he has never come to see us. Perhaps people have been saying something to him about me. You know him, you are always meeting him, couldn't you say or do anything for me?" She looked up with her lips white and drawn. "I feel sometimes as if I were going mad! Oh, it is so terrible to be a woman!" The woman looked down at her. "Now I hear he likes another woman. I don't know who she is, but they say she is so clever, and writes. Oh, it is so terrible, I can't bear it."

The woman leaned her elbow against the mantelpiece, and her face against her hand. She looked down into the fire. Then she turned and looked at the younger woman. "Yes," she said, "it is a very terrible thing to be a woman." She was silent. She said with some difficulty: "Are you sure you love him? Are you sure it is not only the feeling a young girl has for an older man who is celebrated, and of whom every one is talking?"

"I have been nearly mad. I haven't slept for weeks!" She knit her little hands together, till the jewelled rings almost cut into the fingers. "He is everything to me; there is nothing else in the world. You, who are so great, and strong, and clever, and who care only for your work, and for men as your friends, you cannot understand what it is when one person is everything to you, when there is nothing else in the world!"

"And what do you want me to do?"

"Oh, I don't know!" She looked up. "A woman knows what she can do. Don't tell him that I love him." She looked up again. "Just say something to him. Oh, it's so terrible to be a woman; I can't do anything. You won't tell him exactly that I love him? That's the thing that makes a man hate a woman, if you tell it him plainly."

"If I speak to him I must speak openly. He is my friend. I cannot fence with him. I have never fenced with him in my own affairs." She moved as though she were going away from the fireplace, then she turned and said: "Have you thought of what love is between a man and a woman when it means marriage? That long, long life together, day after day, stripped of all romance and distance, living face to face: seeing each other as a man sees his own soul? Do you realise that the end of marriage is to make the man and woman stronger than they were; and that if you cannot, when you are an old man and woman and sit by the fire, say, 'Life has been a braver and a freer thing for us, because we passed it hand in hand, than if we had passed through it alone,' it has failed? Do you care for him enough to live for him, not tomorrow, but when he is an old, faded man, and you an old, faded woman? Can you forgive him his sins and his weaknesses, when they hurt you most? If he were to lie a querulous invalid for twenty years, would you be able to fold him in your arms all that time, and comfort him, as a mother comforts her little child?" The woman drew her breath heavily.

"Oh, I love him absolutely! I would be glad to die, if only I could once know that he loved me better than anything in the world!"

The woman stood looking down at her. "Have you never thought of that other woman; whether *she* could not perhaps make his life as perfect as you?" she asked, slowly.

"Oh, no woman ever could be to him what I would be. I would live for him. He belongs to me." She bent herself forward, not crying, but her shoulders moving. "It is such a terrible thing to be a woman, to be able to do nothing and say nothing!"

The woman put her hand on her shoulder; the younger woman looked up into her face; then the elder turned away and stood looking into the fire. There was such quiet, you could hear the clock tick above the writing-table.

The woman said: "There is one thing I can do for you. I do not know if it will be of any use—I will do it." She turned away.

"Oh, you are so great and good, so beautiful, so different from other women, who are always thinking only of themselves! Thank you so much. I know I can trust you. I couldn't have told my mother, or any one but you."

"Now you must go; I have my work to finish."

The younger woman put her arms round her. "Oh, you are so good and beautiful!"

The silk dress and the fur cloak rustled out of the room.

The woman who was left alone walked up and down, at last faster and faster, till the drops stood on her forehead. After a time she went up to the table; there was written illegibly in a man's hand on a fragment of manuscript paper: *"Can I come to see you this afternoon?"* Near it was a closed and addressed envelope. She opened it. In it were written the words: *"Yes, please, come."*

She tore it across and wrote the words: "No, I shall not be at liberty."

She closed them in an envelope and addressed them. Then she rolled up the manuscript on the table and rang the bell. She gave it to the servant. "Tell the boy to give this to his master, and say the article ends rather abruptly; they must state it is to be continued; I will finish it to-morrow. As he passes No. 20 let him leave this note there."

The servant went out. She walked up and down with her hands folded above her head.

Two months after, the older woman stood before the fire. The door opened suddenly, and the younger woman came in.

"I had to come—I couldn't wait. You have heard, he was married this morning? Oh, do you think it is true? Do help me!" She put out her hands.

"Sit down. Yes, it is quite true."

"Oh, it is so terrible, and I didn't know anything! Did you ever say anything to him?" She caught the woman's hands.

"I never saw him again after the day you were here,—so I could not speak to him,—but I did what I could." She stood looking passively into the fire.

"And they say she is quite a child, only eighteen. They say he only saw her three times before he proposed to her. Do you think it is true?"

"Yes, it is quite true."

"He can't love her. They say he's only marrying her for her rank and her money."

The woman turned quickly.

"What right have you to say that? No one but me knows him. What need has he of any one's rank or wealth? He is greater than them all! Older women may have failed him; he has needed to turn to her beautiful, fresh, young life to compensate him. She is a woman whom any man might have loved, so young and beautiful; her family are famed for their intellect. If he trains her, she may make him a better wife than any other woman would have done."

"Oh, but I can't bear it—I can't bear it!" The younger woman sat down in the chair. "She will be his wife, and have his children."

"Yes." The elder woman moved quickly. "One wants to have the child, and lay its head on one's breast and feed it." She moved quickly. "It would not matter if another woman bore it, if one had it to take care of." She moved restlessly.

"Oh, no, I couldn't bear it to be hers. When I think of her I feel as if I were dying; all my fingers turn cold; I feel dead. Oh, you were only his friend; you don't know!"

The older spoke softly and quickly, "Don't you feel a little gentle to her when you think she's going to be his wife and the mother of his child? I would like to put my arms round her and touch her once, if she would let me. She is so beautiful, they say."

"Oh, I could never bear to see her; it would kill me. And they are so happy together to-day! He is loving her so!"

"Don't you want him to be happy?" The older woman looked down at her. "Have you *never* loved him, at all?"

The younger woman's face was covered with her hands. "Oh, it's so terrible, so dark! and I shall go on living year after year, always in this awful pain! Oh, if I could only die!"

The older woman stood looking into the fire; then slowly and measuredly she said, "There are times, in life, when everything seems dark, when the brain reels, and we cannot see that there is anything but death. But, if we wait long enough, after long, long years, calm comes. It may be we cannot say it was well; but we are contented, we accept the past. The struggle is ended. That day may come for you, perhaps sooner than you think." She spoke slowly and with difficulty.

"No, it can never come for me. If once I have loved a thing, I love it for ever. I can never forget."

"Love is not the only end in life. There are other things to live for."

"Oh, yes, for you! To me love is everything!"

"Now, you must go, dear."

The younger woman stood up. "It has been such a comfort to talk to you. I think I should have killed myself if I had not come. You help me so. I shall always be grateful to you."

The older woman took her hand.

"I want to ask something of you."

"What is it?"

"I cannot quite explain to you. You will not understand. But there are times when something more terrible can come into a life than it should lose what it loves. If you have had a dream of what life ought to be, and you try to make it real, and you fail; and something you have killed out in your heart for long years wakes up and cries, 'Let each man play his own game, and care nothing for the hand of his fellow! Each man for himself. So the game must be played!' and you doubt all you have lived for, and the ground seems washing out under your feet—." She paused. "Such a time has come to me now. If you would promise me that if ever another woman comes to seek your help, you will give it to her, and try to love her for my sake, I think it will help me. I think I should be able to keep my faith."

"Oh, I will do anything you ask me to. You are so good and great."

"Oh, good and great!—if you knew! Now go, dear."

"I have not kept you from your work, have I?"

"No; I have not been working lately. Good-bye, dear."

The younger woman went; and the elder knelt down by the chair, and wailed like a little child when you have struck it and it does not dare to cry loud.

A year after; it was early spring again.

The woman sat at her desk writing; behind her the fire burnt brightly. She was writing a leading article on the causes which in differing peoples lead to the adoption of Free Trade or Protectionist principles.

The woman wrote on quickly. After a while the servant entered and laid a pile of letters on the table. "Tell the boy I shall have done in fifteen minutes." She wrote on. Then she caught sight of the writing on one of the letters. She put down her pen, and opened it. It ran so:—

"DEAR FRIEND,—I am writing to you, because I know you will rejoice to hear of my great happiness. Do you remember how you told me that day by the fire to *wait*, and after long, long years I should see that all was for the best? That time has come sooner than we hoped. Last week in Rome I was married to the best, noblest, most large-hearted of men. We are now in Florence together. You don't know how beautiful all life is to me. I know now that the old passion was only a girl's foolish dream. My husband is the first man I have ever truly loved. He loves me and understands me as no other man ever could. I am thankful that my dream was broken; God had better things in store for me. I don't hate that woman any more; I love every one! How are you, dear? We shall come and see you as soon as we arrive in England. I always think of you so happy in your great work and helping other people. I don't think *now* it is terrible to be a woman; it is lovely.

"I hope you are enjoying this beautiful spring weather.

"Yours, always full of gratitude and love,

"E—."

The woman read the letter: then she stood up and walked towards the fire. She did not re-read it, but stood with it open in her hand, looking down into the blaze. Her lips were drawn in at the corners. Presently she tore the letter up slowly, and watched the bits floating down one by one into the grate. Then she went back to her desk, and began to write, with her mouth still drawn in at the corners. After a while she laid her arm on the paper and her head on her arm, and seemed to go to sleep there.

Presently the servant knocked; the boy was waiting. "Tell him to wait ten minutes more." She took up her pen— "The Policy of the Australian Colonies in favour of Protection is easily understood—" she waited— "when one considers the fact—the fact—;" then she finished the article.

*Cape Town,*
*South Africa, 1892.*

First published in *The New Review* October 1892: 397–403, under the title 'Was it right? - - was it wrong?'

# Stories, Dreams and Allegories

# Preface

*This book contains all of Olive Schreiner's yet unprinted or uncollected imaginative writings, except at least one novel to appear later, which it is proposed to bring forward. They appear unaltered, except in a few minor respects like punctuation, as I found them among her papers.*

*The date and place of writing, affixed by herself, will be found in many of these writings. Regarding the others, I am able to add a few notes. "Who Knocks at the Door?" the latest in date, was published in the* Fortnightly Review *in November 1917. "The Buddhist Priest's Wife" was written at Matjesfontein in 1891 and the following year. "By the Banks of a Full River" probably refers to the "great rains" of 1873, in which year she travelled by coach from Kimberley to Cape Town, but it seems to have been written much later. "The Wax Doll" and "Master Towser," obviously stories for children, were both written when she was a girl; the latter, no doubt revised, was printed in 1881 in the* New College Magazine *(in which also "Dream Life and Real Life" was first printed), her brother being at that time Head Master of New College, Eastbourne; "The Wax Doll" is the most carefully written and preserved of all these manuscripts, but I cannot recall that she ever mentioned it.*

*I desire heartily to thank Mr. Havelock Ellis, my wife's friend and my own, for his kind and valuable help in making this selection.*

S.C. CRONWRIGHT-SCHREINER

*Cape Town, South Africa,*
*October 1922.*

Stories

# Eighteen-ninety-nine

*"Thou fool, that which thou sowest is not quickened unless it die."*

I

It was a warm night: the stars shone down through the thick soft air of the Northern Transvaal into the dark earth, where a little daub-and-wattle house of two rooms lay among the long, grassy slopes.

A light shone through the small window of the house, though it was past midnight. Presently the upper half of the door opened and then the lower, and the tall figure of a woman stepped out into the darkness. She closed the door behind her and walked towards the back of the house where a large round hut stood; beside it lay a pile of stumps and branches quite visible when once the eyes grew accustomed to the darkness. The woman stooped and broke off twigs till she had her apron full, and then returned slowly, and went into the house.

The room to which she returned was a small, bare room, with brown earthen walls and a mud floor; a naked deal table stood in the centre, and a few dark wooden chairs, home-made, with seats of undressed leather, stood round the walls. In the corner opposite the door was an open fireplace, and on the earthen hearth stood an iron three-foot, on which stood a large black kettle, under which coals were smouldering, though the night was hot and close. Against the wall on the left side of the room hung a gun-rack with three guns upon it, and below it a large hunting-watch hung from two nails by its silver chain.

In the corner by the fireplace was a little table with a coffee-pot upon it and a dish containing cups and saucers covered with water, and above it were a few shelves with crockery and a large Bible; but the dim light of the tallow candle which burnt on the table, with its wick of twisted rag, hardly made the corners visible. Beside the table sat a young woman, her head resting on her folded arms, the light of the tallow candle falling full on her head of pale flaxen hair, a little tumbled, and drawn behind into a large knot. The arms crossed on the table, from which the cotton sleeves had fallen back, were the full, rounded arms of one very young.

The older woman, who had just entered, walked to the fireplace, and kneeling down before it took from her apron the twigs and sticks she had gathered and heaped them under the kettle till a blaze sprang up which illumined the whole room. Then she rose up and sat down on a chair before the fire, but facing the table, with her hands crossed on her brown apron.

She was a woman of fifty, spare and broad-shouldered, with black hair, already slightly streaked with grey; from below high, arched eyebrows, and a high forehead, full dark eyes looked keenly, and a sharply cut aquiline nose gave strength to the face; but the mouth below was somewhat sensitive, and not over-full. She crossed and recrossed her knotted hands on her brown apron.

The woman at the table moaned and moved her head from side to side.

"What time is it?" she asked.

The older woman crossed the room to where the hunting-watch hung on the wall.

It showed a quarter-past one, she said, and went back to her seat before the fire, and sat watching the figure beside the table, the firelight bathing her strong upright form and sharp aquiline profile.

Nearly fifty years before her parents had left the Cape Colony, and had set out on the long trek northward, and she, a young child, had been brought with them. She had no remembrance of the colonial home. Her first dim memories were of travelling in an ox-wagon; of dark nights when a fire was lighted in the open air, and people sat round it on the ground, and some faces seemed to stand out more than others in her memory which she thought must be those of her father and mother and of an old grandmother; she could remember lying awake in the back of the wagon while it was moving on, and the stars were shining down on her; and she had a vague memory of great wide plains with buck on them, which she thought must have been in the Free State. But the first thing which sprang out sharp and clear from the past was a day when she and another child, a little boy cousin of her own age, were playing among the bushes on the bank of a stream; she remembered how, suddenly, as they looked through the bushes, they saw black men leap out, and mount the ox-wagon outspanned under the trees; she remembered how they shouted and dragged people along, and stabbed them; she remembered how the blood gushed, and how they, the two young children among the bushes, lay flat on their stomachs and did not move or breathe, with that strange self-preserving instinct found in the young of animals or men who grow up in the open.

She remembered how black smoke came out at the back of the wagon and then red tongues of flame through the top; and even that some of the branches of the tree under which the wagon stood caught fire. She remembered later, when the black men had gone, and it was dark, that they were very hungry, and crept out to where the wagon had stood, and that they looked about on the ground for any scraps of food they might pick up, and that when they could not find any they cried. She remembered nothing clearly after that till some men with large beards and large hats rode up on horseback: it might have been next day or the day after. She remembered how they jumped off their horses and took them up in their arms, and how they cried; but that they, the children, did not cry, they only asked for food. She remembered how one man took a bit of thick, cold roaster-cake out of his pocket, and gave it to her, and how nice it tasted. And she remembered that the men took them up before them on their horses, and that one man tied her close to him with a large red handkerchief.

In the years that came she learnt to know that that which she remembered so clearly was the great and terrible day when, at Weenen, and in the country round, hundreds of women and children and youths and old men fell before the Zulus, and the assegais of Dingaan's braves drank blood.

She learnt that on that day all of her house and name, from the grandmother to the baby in arms, fell, and that she only and the boy cousin, who had hidden with her among the bushes, were left of all her kin in that Northern world. She learnt, too, that the man who tied her to him with the red handkerchief took them back to his wagon, and that he and his wife adopted them, and brought them up among their own children.

She remembered, though less clearly than the day of the fire, how a few years later they trekked away from Natal, and went through great mountain ranges, ranges in and near which lay those places the world was to know later as Laings Nek, and Amajuba, and Ingogo; Elands-laagte, Nicholson Nek, and Spion Kop. She remembered how at last after many wanderings they settled down near the Witwaters Rand,[1] where game was plentiful and wild beasts were dangerous, but there were no natives, and they were far from the English rule.

There the two children grew up among the children of those who had adopted them, and were kindly treated by them as though they were their own; it yet was but natural that these two of the same name and blood should grow up with a peculiar tenderness for each other. And so it came to pass that when they were both eighteen years old they asked consent of the old people, who gave it gladly, that they should marry. For a time the young couple lived on in the house with the old, but after three years they gathered together all their few goods and in their wagon, with their guns and ammunition and a few sheep and cattle, they moved away northwards to found their own home.

For a time they travelled here and travelled there, but at last they settled on a spot where game was plentiful and the soil good, and there among the low undulating slopes, near the bank of a dry sloot, the young man built at last, with his own hands, a little house of two rooms.

On the long slope across the sloot before the house, he ploughed a piece of land and enclosed it, and he built kraals for his stock and so struck root in the land and wandered no more. Those were brave, glad, free days to the young couple. They lived largely on the game which the gun brought down, antelope and wildebeest that wandered even past the doors at night; and now and again a lion was killed: one no farther than the door of the round hut behind the house where the meat and the milk were stored, and two were killed at the kraals. Sometimes, too, traders came with their wagons and in exchange for skins and fine horns sold sugar and coffee and print and tan-cord, and such things as the little household had need of. The lands yielded richly to them, in maize, and pumpkins, and sweet-cane, and melons; and they had nothing to wish for. Then in time three little sons were born to them, who grew as strong and vigorous in the free life of the open veld as the young lions in the long grass

---

1 *Witwaters Rand*— "White water's ridge," now known as the Rand, where Johannesburg and the great mines are situated.

and scrub near the river four miles away. Those were joyous, free years for the man and woman, in which disease, and carking care, and anxiety played no part.

Then came a day when their eldest son was ten years old, and the father went out a-hunting with his Kaffir servants: in the evening they brought him home with a wound eight inches long in his side where a lioness had torn him; they brought back her skin also, as he had shot her at last in the hand-to-throat struggle. He lingered for three days and then died. His wife buried him on the low slope to the left of the house; she and her Kaffir servants alone made the grave and put him in it, for there were no white men near. Then she and her sons lived on there; a new root driven deep into the soil and binding them to it through the grave on the hill-side. She hung her husband's large hunting-watch up on the wall, and put three of his guns over it on the rack, and the gun he had in his hand when he met his death she took down and polished up every day; but one gun she always kept loaded at the head of her bed in the inner room. She counted the stock every night and saw that the Kaffirs ploughed the lands, and she saw to the planting and watering of them herself. Often as the years passed men of the country-side, and even from far off, heard of the young handsome widow who lived alone with her children and saw to her own stock and lands; and they came a-courting. But many of them were afraid to say anything when once they had come, and those who had spoken to her, when once she had answered them, never came again.

About this time too the country-side began to fill in; and people came and settled as near as eight and ten miles away; and as people increased the game began to vanish, and with the game the lions, so that the one her husband killed was almost the last ever seen there. But there was still game enough for food, and when her eldest son was twelve years old, and she gave him his father's smallest gun to go out hunting with, he returned home almost every day with meat enough for the household tied behind his saddle. And as time passed she came also to be known through the country-side as a "wise woman." People came to her to ask advice about their illnesses, or to ask her to dress old wounds that would not heal; and when they questioned her whether she thought the rains would be early, or the game plentiful that year, she was nearly always right. So they called her a "wise woman" because neither she nor they knew any word in that up-country speech of theirs for the thing called "genius." So all things went well till the eldest son was eighteen, and the dark beard was beginning to sprout on his face, and his mother began to think that soon there might be a daughter in the house; for on Saturday evenings, when his work was done, he put on his best clothes and rode off to the next farm eight miles away, where was a young daughter. His mother always saw that he had a freshly ironed shirt waiting for him on his bed, when he came home from the kraals on Saturday nights, and she made plans as to how they would build on two rooms for the new daughter. At this time he was training young horses to have them ready to sell when the traders came round: he was a fine rider and it was always his work. One afternoon he mounted a young horse before the door and it bucked and threw him. He had often fallen before, but this time his neck was broken. He lay dead with his head two feet from his mother's doorstep. They took up his tall, strong body and the next day the neighbours came from the next farm and they buried him beside his father, on the hill-side, and another root was struck into the soil. Then the three who were left in the little farm-house lived and worked on as before, for a year and more.

Then a small native war broke out, and the young burghers of the district were called out to help. The second son was very young, but he was the best shot in the district, so he went away with the others. Three months after the men came back, but among the few who did not return was her son. On a hot sunny afternoon, walking through a mealie field which they thought was deserted and where the dried yellow stalks stood thick, an assegai thrown from an unseen hand found him, and he fell there. His comrades took him and buried him under a large thorn tree, and scraped the earth smooth over him, that his grave might not be found by others. So he was not laid on the rise to the left of the house with his kindred, but his mother's heart went often to that thorn tree in the far north. And now again there were only two in the little mud-house; as there had been years before when the young man and wife first settled there. She and her young lad were always together night and day, and did all that they did together, as though they were mother and daughter. He was a fair lad, tall and gentle as his father had been before him, not huge and dark as his two elder brothers; but he seemed to ripen towards manhood early. When he was only sixteen the thick white down was already gathering heavy on his upper lip; his mother watched him narrowly, and had many thoughts in her heart. One evening as they sat twisting wicks for the candles together, she said to him, "You will be eighteen on your next birthday, my son, that was your father's age when he married me." He said, "Yes," and they spoke no more then. But later in the evening when they sat before the door she said to him: "We are very lonely here. I often long to hear the feet of a little child about the house, and to see one with your father's blood in it play before the door as you and your brothers played. Have you ever thought that you are the last of your father's name and blood left here in the north; that if you died there would be none left?" He said he had thought of it. Then she told him she thought it would be well if he went away, to the part of the country where the people lived who had brought her up: several of the sons and daughters who had grown up with her had now grown up children. He might go down and from among them seek out a young girl whom he liked and who liked him; and if he found her, bring her back as a wife. The lad thought very well of his mother's plan. And when three months were passed, and the ploughing season was over, he rode away one day, on the best black horse they had, his Kaffir boy riding behind him on another, and his mother stood at the gable watching them ride away. For three months she heard nothing of him, for trains were not in those days, and letters came rarely and by chance, and neither he nor she could read or write. One afternoon she stood at the gable end as she always stood when her work was done, looking out along the road that came over the rise, and she saw a large tent-wagon coming along it, and her son walking beside it. She walked to meet it. When she had greeted her son and climbed into the wagon she found there a girl of fifteen with pale flaxen hair and large blue eyes whom he had brought home as his wife. Her father had given her the wagon and oxen as her wedding portion. The older woman's heart wrapt itself about the girl as though she had been the daughter she had dreamed to bear of her own body, and had never borne.

The three lived joyfully at the little house as though they were one person. The young wife had been accustomed to live in a larger house, and down south, where they had things they had not here. She had been to school, and learned to read and write, and she could even talk a little English; but she longed for none of the things which she had had; the little brown house was home enough for her.

After a year a child came, but, whether it were that the mother was too young, it only opened its eyes for an hour on the world and closed them again. The young mother wept bitterly, but her husband folded his arms about her, and the mother comforted both. "You are young, my children, but we shall yet hear the sound of children's voices in the house," she said; and after a little while the young mother was well again and things went on peacefully as before in the little home.

But in the land things were not going on peacefully. That was the time that the flag to escape from which the people had left their old homes in the Colony, and had again left Natal when it followed them there, and had chosen to face the spear of the savage, and the conflict with wild beasts, and death by hunger and thirst in the wilderness rather than live under, had by force and fraud unfurled itself over them again. For the moment a great sullen silence brooded over the land. The people, slow of thought, slow of speech, determined in action, and unforgetting, sat still and waited. It was like the silence that rests over the land before an up-country thunderstorm breaks.

Then words came, "They have not even given us the free government they promised"—then acts—the people rose. Even in that remote country-side the men began to mount their horses, and with their guns ride away to help. In the little mud-house the young wife wept much when he said that he too was going. But when his mother helped him pack his saddle-bags she helped too; and on the day when the men from the next farm went, he rode away also with his gun by his side.

No direct news of the one they had sent away came to the waiting women at the farm-house; then came fleet reports of the victories of Ingogo and Amajuba. Then came an afternoon after he had been gone two months. They had both been to the gable end to look out at the road, as they did continually amid their work, and they had just come in to drink their afternoon coffee when the Kaffir maid ran in to say she saw someone coming along the road who looked like her master. The women ran out. It was the white horse on which he had ridden away, but they almost doubted if it were he. He rode bending on his saddle, with his chin on his breast and his arm hanging at his side. At first they thought he had been wounded, but when they had helped him from his horse and brought him into the house they found it was only a deadly fever which was upon him. He had crept home to them by small stages. Hardly had he any spirit left to tell them of Ingogo, Laings Nek, and Amajuba. For fourteen days he grew worse and on the fifteenth day he died. And the two women buried him where the rest of his kin lay on the hill-side.

And so it came to pass that on that warm starlight night the two women were alone in the little mud-house with the stillness of the veld about them; even their Kaffir servants asleep in their huts beyond the kraals; and the very sheep lying silent in the starlight. They two were alone in the little house, but they knew that before morning they would not be alone, they were awaiting the coming of the dead man's child.

The young woman with her head on the table groaned. "If only my husband were here still," she wailed. The old woman rose and stood beside her, passing her hard, work-worn hand gently over her shoulder as if she were a little child. At last she induced her to go and lie down in the inner room. When she had grown quieter and seemed to have fallen into a light sleep the old woman came to the front room again. It was almost two o'clock and the fire had burned low under the large kettle. She scraped the coals together and went out of the front door to fetch more wood, and closed the door behind her. The night air struck cool and fresh upon her face after the close air of the house, the stars seemed to be growing lighter as the night advanced, they shot down their light as from a million polished steel points. She walked to the back of the house where, beyond the round hut that served as a store-room, the wood-pile lay. She bent down gathering sticks and chips till her apron was full, then slowly she raised herself and stood still. She looked upwards. It was a wonderful night. The white band of the Milky Way crossed the sky overhead, and from every side stars threw down their light, sharp as barbed spears, from the velvety blue-black of the sky. The woman raised her hand to her forehead as if pushing the hair farther off it, and stood motionless, looking up. After a long time she dropped her hand and began walking slowly towards the house. Yet once or twice on the way she paused and stood looking up. When she went into the house the woman in the inner room was again moving and moaning. She laid the sticks down before the fire and went into the next room. She bent down over the bed where the younger woman lay, and put her hand upon her. "My daughter," she said slowly, "be comforted. A wonderful thing has happened to me. As I stood out in the starlight it was as though a voice came down to me and spoke. The child which will be born of you to-night will be a man-child and he will live to do great things for his land and for his people."

Before morning there was the sound of a little wail in the mud-house: and the child who was to do great things for his land and for his people was born.

## II

Six years passed; and all was as it had been at the little house among the slopes. Only a new piece of land had been ploughed up and added to the land before the house, so that the ploughed land now almost reached to the ridge.

The young mother had grown stouter, and lost her pink and white; she had become a working-woman, but she still had the large knot of flaxen hair behind her head and the large wondering eyes. She had many suitors in those six years, but she sent them all away. She said the old woman looked after the farm as well as any man might, and her son would be grown up by and by. The grandmother's hair was a little more streaked with grey, but it was as thick as ever, and her shoulders as upright; only some of her front teeth had fallen out, which made her lips close more softly.

The great change was that wherever the women went there was the flaxen-haired child to walk beside them holding on to their skirts or clasping their hands.

The neighbours said they were ruining the child: they let his hair grow long, like a girl's, because it curled; and they never let him wear velschoens like other children but always shop boots; and his mother sat up at night to iron his pinafores as if the next day were always a Sunday.

But the women cared nothing for what was said; to them he was not as any other child. He asked them strange questions they could not answer, and he never troubled them by wishing to go and play with the little Kaffirs as other children trouble. When neighbours came over and brought their children with them he ran away and hid in the sloot to play by himself till they were gone. No, he was not like other children!

When the women went to lie down on hot days after dinner sometimes, he would say that he did not want to sleep; but he would not run about and make a noise like other children—he would go and sit outside in the shade of the house, on the front door-step, quite still, with his little hands resting on his knees, and stare far away at the ploughed lands on the slope, or the shadows nearer; the women would open the bedroom window, and peep out to look at him as he sat there.

The child loved his mother and followed her about to the milk house, and to the kraals; but he loved his grandmother best.

She told him stories.

When she went to the lands to see how the Kaffirs were ploughing he would run at her side holding her dress; when they had gone a short way he would tug gently at it and say, "Grandmother, tell me things!"

And long before day broke, when it was yet quite dark, he would often creep from the bed where he slept with his mother into his grandmother's bed in the corner; he would put his arms round her neck and stroke her face till she woke, and then whisper softly, "Tell me stories!" and she would tell them to him in a low voice not to wake the mother, till the cock crowed and it was time to get up and light the candle and the fire.

But what he liked best of all were the hot, still summer nights, when the women put their chairs before the door because it was too warm to go to sleep; and he would sit on the stoof at his grandmother's feet and lean his head against her knees, and she would tell him on and on of the things he liked to hear; and he would watch the stars as they slowly set along the ridge, or the moonlight, casting bright-edged shadows from the gable as she talked. Often after the mother had got sleepy and gone in to bed the two sat there together.

The stories she told him were always true stories of the things she had seen or of things she had heard. Sometimes they were stories of her own childhood: of the day when she and his grandfather hid among the bushes, and saw the wagon burnt; sometimes they were of the long trek from Natal to the Transvaal; sometimes of the things which happened to her and his grandfather when first they came to that spot among the ridges, of how there was no house there nor lands, only two bare grassy slopes when they outspanned their wagon there the first night; she told of a lion she once found when she opened the door in the morning, sitting, with paws crossed, upon the threshold, and how the grandfather jumped out of bed and reopened the door two inches, and shot it through the opening; the skin was kept in the round storehouse still, very old and mangy.

Sometimes she told him of the two uncles who were dead, and of his own father, and of all they had been and done. But sometimes she told him of things much farther off: of the old Colony where she had been born, but which she could not remember, and of the things which happened there in the old days. She told him of how the British had taken the Cape over, and of how the English had hanged their men at the "Slachters Nek" for resisting the English Government, and of how the friends and relations had been made to stand round to see them hanged whether they would or no, and of how the scaffold broke down as they were being hanged, and the people looking on cried aloud, "It is the finger of God! They are saved!" but how the British hanged them up again. She told him of the great trek in which her parents had taken part to escape from under the British flag; of the great battles with Moselikatse; and of the murder of Retief and his men by Dingaan, and of Dingaan's Day. She told him how the British Government followed them into Natal, and of how they trekked north and east to escape from it again; and she told him of the later things, of the fight at Laings Nek, and Ingogo, and Amajuba, where his father had been. Always she told the same story in exactly the same words over and over again, till the child knew them all by heart, and would ask for this and then that.

The story he loved best, and asked for more often than all the others, made his grandmother wonder, because it did not seem to her the story a child would best like; it was not a story of lion-hunting, or wars, or adventures. Continually when she asked what she should tell him, he said, "About the mountains!"

It was the story of how the Boer women in Natal when the English Commissioner came to annex their country, collected to meet him and pointing toward the Drakens Berg Mountains said, "We go across those mountains to freedom or to death!"

More than once, when she was telling him the story, she saw him stretch out his little arm and raise his hand, as though he were speaking.

One evening as he and his mother were coming home from the milking kraals, and it was getting dark, and he was very tired, having romped about shouting among the young calves and kids all the evening, he held her hand tightly.

"Mother," he said suddenly, "when I am grown up, I am going to Natal."

"Why, my child!" she asked him; "there are none of our family living there now."

He waited a little, then said, very slowly, "I am going to go and try to get our land back!"

His mother started; if there were one thing she was more firmly resolved on in her own mind than any other it was that he should never go to the wars. She began to talk quickly of the old white cow who had kicked the pail over as she was milked, and when she got to the house she did not even mention to the grandmother what had happened; it seemed better to forget.

One night in the rainy season when it was damp and chilly they sat round the large fireplace in the front room.

Outside the rain was pouring in torrents and you could hear the water rushing in the great dry sloot before the door. His grandmother, to amuse him, had sprung some dried mealies in the great black pot and sprinkled them with sugar, and now he sat on the stoof at her feet with a large lump of the sticky sweetmeat in his hand, watching the fire. His grandmother from above him was watching it also, and his mother in her elbow-chair on the other side of the fire had her eyes half closed and was nodding already with the warmth of the room and her long day's work. The child sat so quiet, the hand with the lump of sweetmeat resting on his knee, that his grandmother thought he had gone to sleep too. Suddenly he said without looking up, "Grandmother?"

"Yes."

He waited rather a long time, then said slowly, "Grandmother, did God make the English too?"

She also waited for a while, then she said, "Yes, my child; He made all things."

They were silent again, and there was no sound but of the rain falling and the fire cracking and the sloot rushing outside. Then he threw his head backwards on to his grandmother's knee and looking up into her face, said, "But, grandmother, why did He make them?"

Then she too was silent for a long time. "My child," at last she said, "we cannot judge the ways of the Almighty. He does that which seems good in His own eyes."

The child sat up and looked back at the fire. Slowly he tapped his knee with the lump of sweetmeat once or twice; then he began to munch it; and soon the mother started wide awake and said it was time for all to go to bed.

The next morning his grandmother sat on the front doorstep cutting beans in an iron basin; he sat beside her on the step pretending to cut too, with a short, broken knife. Presently he left off and rested his hands on his knees, looking away at the hedge beyond, with his small forehead knit tight between the eyes.

"Grandmother," he said suddenly, in a small, almost shrill voice, "do the English want *all* the lands of *all* the people?"

The handle of his grandmother's knife as she cut clinked against the iron side of the basin. "All they can get," she said.

After a while he made a little movement almost like a sigh, and took up his little knife again and went on cutting.

Some time after that, when a trader came by, his grandmother bought him a spelling-book and a slate and pencils, and his mother began to teach him to read and write. When she had taught him for a year he knew all she did. Sometimes when she was setting him a copy and left a letter out in a word, he would quietly take the pencil when she set it down and put the letter in, not with any idea of correcting her, but simply because it must be there.

Often at night when the child had gone to bed early, tired out with his long day's play, and the two women were left in the front room with the tallow candle burning on the table between them, then they talked of his future.

Ever since he had been born everything they had earned had been put away in the wagon chest under the grandmother's bed. When the traders with their wagons came round the women bought nothing except a few groceries and clothes for the child; even before they bought a yard of cotton print for a new apron they talked long and solemnly as to whether the old one might not be made to do by repatching; and they mixed much more dry pumpkin and corn with their coffee than before he was born. It was to earn more money that the large new piece of land had been added to the lands before the house.

They were going to have him educated. First he was to be taught all they could at home, then to be sent away to a great school in the old Colony, and then he was to go over the sea to Europe and come back an advocate or a doctor or a parson. The grandmother had made a long journey to the next town, to find out from the minister just how much it would cost to do it all.

In the evenings when they sat talking it over the mother generally inclined to his becoming a parson. She never told the grandmother why, but the real reason was because parsons do not go to the wars. The grandmother generally favoured his becoming an advocate, because he might become a judge. Sometimes they sat discussing these matters till the candle almost burnt out.

"Perhaps, one day," the mother would at last say, "he may yet become President!"

Then the grandmother would slowly refold her hands across her apron and say softly, "Who knows?—who knows?"

Often they would get the box out from under the bed (looking carefully across to the corner to see he was fast asleep) and would count out all the money, though each knew to a farthing how much was there; then they would make it into little heaps, so much for this, so much for that, and then they would count on their fingers how many good seasons it would take to make the rest, and how old he would be.

When he was eight and had learnt all his mother could teach him, they sent him to school every day on an adjoining farm six miles off, where the people had a schoolmaster. Every day he rode over on the great white horse his father went to the wars with; his mother was afraid to let him ride alone at first, but his grandmother said he must learn to do everything alone. At four o'clock when he came back one or other of the women was always looking out to see the little figure on the tall horse coming over the ridge.

When he was eleven they gave him his father's smallest gun; and one day not long after he came back with his first small buck. His mother had the skin dressed and bound with red, and she laid it as a mat under the table, and even the horns she did not throw away, and saved them in the round house, because it was his first.

When he was fourteen the schoolmaster said he could teach him no more; that he ought to go to some larger school where they taught Latin and other difficult things; they had not yet money enough and he was not quite old enough to go to the old Colony, so they sent him first to the High-veld, where his mother's relations lived and where there were good schools, where they taught the difficult things; he could live with his mother's relations and come back once a year for the holidays.

They were great times when he came.

His mother made him koekies [1] and sasarties [2] and nice things every day; and he used to sit on the stoof at her feet and let her play with his hair like when he was quite small. With his grandmother he talked. He tried to explain to her all he was learning, and he read the English newspapers to her (she could neither read in English nor Dutch), translating them. Most of all she liked his Atlas. They would sometimes sit over it for half an hour in the evening tracing the different lands and talking of them. On the warm nights he used still to sit outside on the stoof at her feet with his head against her knee, and they used to discuss things that were happening in other lands and in South Africa; and sometimes they sat there quite still together.

It was now he who had the most stories to tell; he had seen Krugersdorp, and Johannesburg, and Pretoria; he knew the world; he was at Krugersdorp when Dr. Jameson made his raid. Sometimes he sat for an hour, telling her of things, and she sat quietly listening.

When he was seventeen, nearly eighteen, there was money enough in the box to pay for his going to the Colony and then to Europe; and he came home to spend a few months with them before he went.

He was very handsome now; not tall, and very slight, but with fair hair that curled close to his head, and white hands like a town's man. All the girls in the country-side were in love with him. They all wished he would come and see them. But he seldom rode from home except to go to the next farm where he had been at school. There lived little Aletta, who was the daughter of the woman his uncle had loved before he went to the Kaffir war and got killed. She was only fifteen years old, but they had always been great friends. She netted him a purse of green silk. He said he would take it with him to Europe, and

1 *Koekies*: little cakes.
2 *Sasarties*: meat prepared in a certain way.

would show it her when he came back and was an advocate; and he gave her a book with her name written in it, which she was to show to him.

These were the days when the land was full of talk; it was said the English were landing troops in South Africa, and wanted to have war. Often the neighbours from the nearest farms would come to talk about it (there were more farms now, the country was filling in, and the nearest railway station was only a day's journey off), and they discussed matters. Some said they thought there would be war; others again laughed, and said it would be only Jameson and his white flag again. But the grandmother shook her head, and if they asked her, "Why," she said, "it will not be the war of a week, nor of a month; if it comes it will be the war of years," but she would say nothing more.

Yet sometimes when she and her grandson were walking along together in the lands she would talk.

Once she said: "It is as if a great heavy cloud hung just above my head, as though I wished to press it back with my hands and could not. It will be a great war—a great war. Perhaps the English Government will take the land for a time, but they will not keep it. The gold they have fought for will divide them, till they slay one another over it."

Another day she said: "This land will be a great land one day with one people from the sea to the north—but we shall not live to see it."

He said to her: "But how can that be when we are all of different races?"

She said: "The land will make us one. Were not our fathers of more than one race?"

Another day, when she and he were sitting by the table after dinner, she pointed to a sheet of exercise paper, on which he had been working out a problem and which was covered with algebraical symbols, and said, "In fifteen years' time the Government of England will not have one piece of land in all South Africa as large as that sheet of paper."

One night when the milking had been late and she and he were walking down together from the kraals in the starlight she said to him: "If this war comes let no man go to it lightly, thinking he will surely return home, nor let him go expecting victory on the next day. It will come at last, but not at first." "Sometimes," she said, "I wake at night and it is as though the whole house were filled with smoke—and I have to get up and go outside to breathe. It is as though I saw my whole land blackened and desolate. But when I look up it is as though a voice cried out to me, 'Have no fear!'"

They were getting his things ready for him to go away after Christmas. His mother was making him shirts and his grandmother was having a kaross of jackals' skins made that he might take it with him to Europe where it was so cold. But his mother noticed that whenever the grandmother was in the room with him and he was not looking at her, her eyes were always curiously fixed on him as though they were questioning something. The hair was growing white and a little thin over her temples now; but her eyes were as bright as ever, and she could do a day's work with any man.

One day when the youth was at the kraals helping the Kaffir boys to mend a wall, and the mother was kneading bread in the front room, and the grandmother washing up the breakfast things, the son of the Field-Cornet came riding over from his father's farm, which was about twelve miles off. He stopped at the kraal and Jan and he stood talking for some time, then they walked down to the farmhouse, the Kaffir boy leading the horse behind them. Jan stopped at the round store, but the Field-Cornet's son went to the front door. The grandmother asked him in, and handed him some coffee, and the mother, her hands still in the dough, asked him how things were going at his father's farm, and if his mother's young turkeys had come out well, and she asked if he had met Jan at the kraals. He answered the questions slowly, and sipped his coffee. Then he put the cup down on the table; and said suddenly in the same measured voice, staring at the wall in front of him, that war had broken out, and his father had sent him round to call out all fighting burghers.

The mother took her hands out of the dough and stood upright beside the trough as though paralysed. Then she cried in a high, hard voice, unlike her own, "Yes, but Jan cannot go! He is hardly eighteen! He's got to go and be educated in other lands! You can't take the only son of a widow!"

"Aunt," said the young man slowly, "no one will make him go."

The grandmother stood resting the knuckles of both hands on the table, her eyes fixed on the young man. "He shall decide himself," she said.

The mother wiped her hands from the dough and rushed past them and out at the door; the grandmother followed slowly.

They found him in the shade at the back of the house, sitting on a stump; he was cleaning the belt of his new Mauser which lay across his knees.

"Jan," his mother cried, grasping his shoulder, "you are not going away? You can't go! You must stay. You can go by Delagoa Bay if there is fighting on the other side! There is plenty of money!"

He looked softly up into her face with his blue eyes. "We have all to be at the Field Cornet's at nine o'clock to-morrow morning," he said. She wept aloud and argued.

His grandmother turned slowly without speaking, and went back into the house. When she had given the Field Cornet's son another cup of coffee, and shaken hands with him, she went into the bedroom and opened the box in which her grandson's clothes were kept, to see which things he should take with him. After a time the mother came back too. He had kissed her and talked to her until she too had at last said it was right he should go.

All day they were busy. His mother baked him biscuits to take in his bag, and his grandmother made a belt of two strips of leather; she sewed them together herself and put a few sovereigns between the stitchings. She said some of his comrades might need the money if he did not.

The next morning early he was ready. There were two saddle-bags tied to his saddle and before it was strapped the kaross his grandmother had made; she said it would be useful when he had to sleep on damp ground. When he had greeted them, he rode away towards the rise: and the women stood at the gable of the house to watch him.

When he had gone a little way he turned in his saddle, and they could see he was smiling; he took off his hat and waved it in the air; the early morning sunshine made his hair as yellow as the tassels that hang from the head of ripening mealies. His mother covered her face with the sides of her kappie and wept aloud; but the grandmother shaded her eyes with both her hands and stood watching him till the figure passed out of sight over the ridge; and when it was gone and the mother returned to the house crying, she still stood watching the line against the sky.

The two women were very quiet during the next days, they worked hard, and seldom spoke. After eight days there came a long letter from him (there was now a post once a week from the station to the Field Cornet's). He said he was well and in very good spirits. He had been to Krugersdorp, and Johannesburg, and Pretoria; all the family living there were well and sent greetings. He had joined a corps that was leaving for the front the next day. He sent also a long message to Aletta, asking them to tell her he was sorry to go away without saying good-bye; and he told his mother how good the biscuits and biltong were she had put into his saddle-bag; and he sent her a piece of "vier-kleur" ribbon in the letter, to wear on her breast.

The women talked a great deal for a day or two after this letter came. Eight days after there was a short note from him, written in pencil in the train on his way to the front. He said all was going well, and if he did not write soon they were not to be anxious; he would write as often as he could.

For some days the women discussed that note too.

Then came two weeks without a letter, the two women became very silent. Every day they sent the Kaffir boy over to the Field Cornet's, even on the days when there was no post, to hear if there was any news.

Many reports were flying about the country-side. Some said that an English armoured train had been taken on the western border; that there had been fighting at Albertina, and in Natal. But nothing seemed quite certain.

Another week passed.... Then the two women became very quiet.

The grandmother, when she saw her daughter-in-law left the food untouched on her plate, said there was no need to be anxious; men at the front could not always find paper and pencils to write with and might be far from any post office. Yet night after night she herself would rise from her bed saying she felt the house close, and go and walk up and down outside.

Then one day suddenly all their servants left them except one Kaffir and his wife, whom they had had for years, and the servants from the farms about went also, which was a sign there had been news of much fighting; for the Kaffirs hear things long before the white man knows them.

Three days after, as the women were clearing off the breakfast things, the youngest son of the Field-Cornet, who was only fifteen and had not gone to the war with the others, rode up. He hitched his horse to the post, and came towards the door. The mother stepped forward to meet him and shook hands in the doorway.

"I suppose you have come for the carrot seed I promised your mother? I was not able to send it, as our servants ran away," she said, as she shook his hand. "There isn't a letter from Jan, is there?" The lad said no, there was no letter from him, and shook hands with the grandmother. He stood by the table instead of sitting down.

The mother turned to the fireplace to get coals to put under the coffee to rewarm it; but the grandmother stood leaning forward with her eyes fixed on him from across the table. He felt uneasily in his breast pocket.

"Is there no news?" the mother said without looking round, as she bent over the fire.

"Yes, there is news, Aunt."

She rose quickly and turned towards him, putting down the brazier on the table. He took a letter out of his breast pocket. "Aunt, my father said I must bring this to you. It came inside one to him and they asked him to send one of us over with it."

The mother took the letter; she held it, examining the address.

"It looks to me like the writing of Sister Annie's Paul," she said. "Perhaps there is news of Jan in it"—she turned to them with a half-nervous smile— "they were always such friends."

"All is as God wills, Aunt," the young man said, looking down fixedly at the top of his riding-whip.

But the grandmother leaned forward motionless, watching her daughter-in-law as she opened the letter.

She began to read to herself, her lips moving slowly as she deciphered it word by word.

Then a piercing cry rang through the roof of the little mud-farm-house.

"He is dead! My boy is dead!"

She flung the letter on the table and ran out at the front door.

Far out across the quiet ploughed lands and over the veld to where the kraals lay the cry rang. The Kaffir woman who sat outside her hut beyond the kraals nursing her baby heard it and came down with her child across her hip to see what was the matter. At the side of the round house she stood motionless and open-mouthed, watching the woman, who paced up and down behind the house with her apron thrown over her head and her hands folded above it, crying aloud.

In the front room the grandmother, who had not spoken since he came, took up the letter and put it in the lad's hands. "Read," she whispered.

And slowly the lad spelled it out.

"MY DEAR AUNT,

"I hope this letter finds you well. The Commandant has asked me to write it.

"We had a great fight four days ago, and Jan is dead. The Commandant says I must tell you how it happened. Aunt, there were five of us first in a position on that koppie, but two got killed, and then there were only three of us—Jan, and I, and Uncle Peter's Frikkie.

Aunt, the khakies[1] were coming on all round just like locusts, and the bullets were coming just like hail. It was bare on that side of the koppie where we were, but we had plenty of cartridges. We three took up a position where there were some small stones and we fought, Aunt; we had to. One bullet took off the top of my ear, and Jan got two bullets, one through the flesh in the left leg and one through his arm, but he could still fire his gun. Then we three meant to go to the top of the koppie, but a bullet took Jan right through his chest. We knew he couldn't go any farther. The khakies were right at the foot of the koppie just coming up. He told us to lay him down, Aunt. We said we would stay by him, but he said we must go. I put my jacket under his head and Frikkie put his over his feet. We threw his gun far away from him that they might see how it was with him. He said he hadn't much pain, Aunt. He was full of blood from his arm, but there wasn't much from his chest, only a little out of the corners of his mouth. He said we must make haste or the khakies would catch us; he said he wasn't afraid to be left there.

"Aunt, when we got to the top, it was all full of khakies like the sea on the other side, all among the koppies and on our koppie too. We were surrounded, Aunt; the last I saw of Frikkie he was sitting on a stone with the blood running down his face, but he got under a rock and hid there; some of our men found him next morning and brought him to camp. Aunt, there was a khakie's horse standing just below where I was, with no one on it. I jumped on and rode. The bullets went this way and the bullets went that, but I rode! Aunt, the khakies were sometimes as near me as that tent-pole, only the Grace of God saved me. It was dark in the night when I got back to where our people were, because I had to go round all the koppies to get away from the khakies.

"Aunt, the next day we went to look for him. We found him where we left him; but he was turned over on to his face; they had taken all his things, his belt and his watch, and the pugaree from his hat, even his boots. The little green silk purse he used to carry we found on the ground by him, but nothing in it. I will send it back to you whenever I get an opportunity.

"Aunt, when we turned him over on his back there were four bayonet stabs in his body. The doctor says it was only the first three while he was alive; the last one was through his heart and killed him at once.

"We gave him Christian burial, Aunt; we took him to the camp.

"The Commandant was there, and all of the family who are with the Commando were there, and they all said they hoped God would comfort you." ...

The old woman leaned forward and grasped the boy's arm. "Read it over again," she said, "from where they found him." He turned back and re-read

---

1 *Khakies*: soldiers.

slowly. She gazed at the page as though she were reading also. Then, suddenly, she slipped out at the front door.

At the back of the house she found her daughter-in-law still walking up and down, and the Kaffir woman with a red handkerchief bound round her head and the child sitting across her hip, sucking from her long, pendulous breast, looking on.

The old woman walked up to her daughter-in-law and grasped her firmly by the arm.

"He's dead! You know, my boy's dead!" she cried, drawing the apron down with her right hand and disclosing her swollen and bleared face. "Oh, his beautiful hair—Oh, his beautiful hair!"

The old woman held her arm tighter with both hands; the younger opened her half-closed eyes, and looked into the keen, clear eyes fixed on hers, and stood arrested.

The old woman drew her face closer to hers. "You ... do ... not ... know ... what ... has ... happened!" she spoke slowly, her tongue striking her front gum, the jaw moving stiffly, as though partly paralysed. She loosed her left hand and held up the curved work-worn fingers before her daughter-in-law's face. "Was it not told me ... the night he was born ... here ... at this spot ... that he would do great things ... great things ... for his land and his people?" She bent forward till her lips almost touched the other's. "Three ... bullet ... wounds ... and four ... bayonet ... stabs!" She raised her left hand high in the air. "Three ... bullet ... wounds ... and four ... bayonet ... stabs! ... Is it given to many to die so for their land and their people!"

The younger woman gazed into her eyes, her own growing larger and larger. She let the old woman lead her by the arm in silence into the house.

The Field-Cornet's son was gone, feeling there was nothing more to be done; and the Kaffir woman went back with her baby to her hut beyond the kraals. All day the house was very silent. The Kaffir woman wondered that no smoke rose from the farm-house chimney, and that she was not called to churn, or wash the pots. At three o'clock she went down to the house. As she passed the grated window of the round out-house she saw the buckets of milk still standing unsifted [1] on the floor as they had been set down at breakfast time, and under the great soap-pot beside the wood pile the fire had died out. She went round to the front of the house and saw the door and window shutters still closed, as though her mistresses were still sleeping. So she rebuilt the fire under the soap-pot and went back to her hut.

It was four o'clock when the grandmother came out from the dark inner room where she and her daughter-in-law had been lying down; she opened the top of the front door, and lit the fire with twigs, and set the large black kettle over it. When it boiled she made coffee, and poured out two cups and set them on the table with a plate of biscuits, and then called her daughter-in-law from the inner room.

The two women sat down one on each side of the table, with their coffee

---

1 *Unsifted*: unstrained.

cups before them, and the biscuits between them, but for a time they said nothing, but sat silent, looking out through the open door at the shadow of the house and the afternoon sunshine beyond it. At last the older woman motioned that the younger should drink her coffee. She took a little, and then folding her arms on the table rested her head on them, and sat motionless as if asleep.

The older woman broke up a biscuit into her own cup, and stirred it round and round; and then, without tasting, sat gazing out into the afternoon's sunshine till it grew cold beside her.

It was five, and the heat was quickly dying; the glorious golden colouring of the later afternoon was creeping over everything when she rose from her chair. She moved to the door and took from behind it two large white calico bags hanging there, and from nails on the wall she took down two large brown cotton kappies. She walked round the table and laid her hand gently on her daughter-in-law's arm. The younger woman raised her head slowly and looked up into her mother-in-law's face; and then, suddenly, she knew that her mother-in-law was an old, old, woman. The little shrivelled face that looked down at her was hardly larger than a child's, the eyelids were half closed and the lips worked at the corners and the bones cut out through the skin in the temples.

"I am going out to sow—the ground will be getting too dry to-morrow; will you come with me?" she said gently.

The younger woman made a movement with her hand, as though she said "What is the use?" and redropped her hand on the table.

"It may go on for long, our burghers must have food," the old woman said gently.

The younger woman looked into her face, then she rose slowly and taking one of the brown kappies from her hand, put it on, and hung one of the bags over her left arm; the old woman did the same and together they passed out of the door. As the older woman stepped down the younger caught her and saved her from falling.

"Take my arm, mother," she said.

But the old woman drew her shoulders up. "I only stumbled a little!" she said quickly. "That step has been always too high"; but before she reached the plank over the sloot the shoulders had drooped again, and the neck fallen forward.

The mould in the lands was black and soft; it lay in long ridges, as it had been ploughed up a week before, but the last night's rain had softened it and made it moist and ready for putting in the seed.

The bags which the women carried on their arms were full of the seed of pumpkins and mealies. They began to walk up the lands, keeping parallel with the low hedge of dried bushes that ran up along the side of the sloot almost up to the top of the ridge. At every few paces they stopped and bent down to press into the earth, now one and then the other kind of seed from their bags. Slowly they walked up and down till they reached the top of the land almost on the horizon line; and then they turned, and walked down, sowing as they went. When they had reached the bottom of the land before the farm-house it was almost sunset, and their bags were nearly empty; but they turned to go up once more. The light of the setting sun cast long, gaunt shadows from their figures across the ploughed land, over the low hedge and the sloot, into the bare veld beyond; shadows that grew longer and longer as they passed slowly on pressing in the seeds ... The seeds! ... that were to lie in the dank, dark, earth, and rot there, seemingly, to die, till their outer covering had split and fallen from them ... and then, when the rains had fallen, and the sun had shone, to come up above the earth again, and high in the clear air to lift their feathery plumes and hang out their pointed leaves and silken tassels! To cover the ground with a mantle of green and gold through which sunlight quivered, over which the insects hung by thousands, carrying yellow pollen on their legs and wings and making the air alive with their hum and stir, while grain and fruit ripened surely ... for the next season's harvest!

When the sun had set, the two women with their empty bags turned and walked silently home in the dark to the farm-house.

# Nineteen hundred and one

Near one of the camps in the Northern Transvaal are the graves of two women. The older one died first, on the twenty-third of the month, from hunger and want; the younger woman tended her with ceaseless care and devotion till the end. A week later when the British Superintendent came round to inspect the tents, she was found lying on her blanket on the mud-floor dead, with the rations of bread and meat she had got four days before untouched on a box beside her. Whether she died of disease, or from inability to eat the food, no one could say. Some who had seen her said she hardly seemed to care to live after the old woman died; they buried them side by side.

There is no stone and no name upon either grave to say who lies there ... our unknown ... our unnamed ... our forgotten dead.

# In the year nineteen hundred and four

If you look for the little farm-house among the ridges you will not find it there to-day.

The English soldiers burnt it down. You can only see where the farm-house once stood, because the stramonia and weeds grow high and very strong there; and where the ploughed lands were you can only tell, because the veld never grows quite the same on land that has once been ploughed. Only a brown patch among the long grass on the ridge shows where the kraals and huts once were.

In a country house in the north of England the owner has upon his wall an old flint-lock gun. He takes it down to show his friends. It is a small thing he picked up in the war in South Africa, he says. It must be at least eighty years old and is very valuable. He shows how curiously it is constructed; he says it must have been kept in such perfect repair by continual polishing for the steel shines as if it were silver. He does not tell that he took it from the wall of the little mud house before he burnt it down.

It was the grandfather's gun, which the women had kept polished on the wall.

In a London drawing-room the descendant of a long line of titled forefathers entertains her guests. It is a fair room, and all that money can buy to make life soft and beautiful is there.

On the carpet stands a little dark wooden stoof. When one of her guests notices it, she says it is a small curiosity which her son brought home to her from South Africa when he was out in the war there; and how good it was of him to think of her when he was away in the back country. And when they ask what it is, she says it is a thing Boer women have as a footstool and to keep their feet warm; and she shows the hole at the side where they put the coals in, and the little holes at the top where the heat comes out.

And the other woman puts her foot out and rests it on the stoof just to try how it feels, and drawls "How f-u-n-n-y!"

It is grandmother's stoof, that the child used to sit on.

The wagon chest was found and broken open just before the thatch caught fire, by three private soldiers, and they divided the money between them; one spent his share in drink, another had his stolen from him, but the third sent his home to England to a girl in the East End of London. With part of it she bought a gold brooch and ear-rings, and the rest she saved to buy a silk wedding-dress when he came home.

A syndicate of Jews in Johannesburg and London have bought the farm. They purchased it from the English Government, because they think to find gold on it. They have purchased it and paid for it ... but they do not possess it.

Only the men who lie in their quiet graves upon the hill-side, who lived on it, and loved it, possess it; and the piles of stones above them, from among the long waving grasses, keep watch over the land.

# The Buddhist Priest's Wife

Cover her up! How still it lies! You can see the outline under the white. You would think she was asleep. Let the sunshine come in; it loved it so. She that had travelled so far, in so many lands, and done so much and seen so much, how she must like rest now! Did she ever love anything absolutely, this woman whom so many men loved, and so many women; who gave so much sympathy and never asked for anything in return! did she ever need a love she could not have? Was she never obliged to unclasp her fingers from anything to which they clung? Was she really so strong as she looked? Did she never wake up in the night crying for that which she could not have? Were thought and travel enough for her? Did she go about for long days with a weight that crushed her to earth? Cover her up! I do not think she would have liked us to look at her. In one way she was alone all her life; she would have liked to be alone now!... Life must have been very beautiful to her, or she would not look so young now. Cover her up! Let us go!

\*    \*    \*    \*    \*    \*

Many years ago in a London room, up long flights of stairs, a fire burnt up in a grate. It showed the marks on the walls where pictures had been taken down, and the little blue flowers in the wall-paper and the blue felt carpet on the floor, and a woman sat by the fire in a chair at one side.

Presently the door opened, and the old woman came in who took care of the entrance hall downstairs.

"Do you not want anything to-night?" she said.

"No, I am only waiting for a visitor; when they have been, I shall go."

"Have you got all your things taken away already?"

"Yes, only these I am leaving."

The old woman went down again, but presently came up with a cup of tea in her hand.

"You must drink that; it's good for one. Nothing helps one like tea when one's been packing all day."

The young woman at the fire did not thank her, but she ran her hand over the old woman's from the wrist to the fingers.

"I'll say good-bye to you when I go out."

The woman poked the fire, put the last coals on, and went.

When she had gone the young one did not drink the tea, but drew her little silver cigarette case from her pocket and lighted a cigarette. For a while she sat smoking by the fire; then she stood up and walked the room.

When she had paced for a while she sat down again beside the fire. She threw the end of her cigarette away into the fire, and then began to walk again with her hands behind her. Then she went back to her seat and lit another cigarette, and paced again. Presently she sat down, and looked into the fire; she pressed the palms of her hands together, and then sat quietly staring into it.

Then there was a sound of feet on the stairs and someone knocked at the door.

She rose and threw the end into the fire and said without moving, "Come in."

The door opened and a man stood there in evening dress. He had a great-coat on, open in front.

"May I come in? I couldn't get rid of this downstairs; I didn't see where to leave it!" He took his coat off. "How are you? This is a real bird's nest!"

She motioned to a chair.

"I hope you did not mind my asking you to come?"

"Oh no, I am delighted. I only found your note at my club twenty minutes ago."

He sat down on a chair before the fire.

"So you really are going to India? How delightful! But what are you to do there? I think it was Grey told me six weeks ago you were going, but regarded it as one of those mythical stories which don't deserve credence. Yet I'm sure I don't know! Why, nothing would surprise me."

He looked at her in a half-amused, half-interested way.

"What a long time it is since we met! Six months, eight?"

"Seven," she said.

"I really thought you were trying to avoid me. What have you been doing with yourself all this time?"

"Oh, been busy. Won't you have a cigarette?"

She held out the little case to him.

"Won't you take one yourself? I know you object to smoking with men, but you can make an exception in my case!"

"Thank you." She lit her own and passed him the matches.

"But really what have you been doing with yourself all this time? You've entirely disappeared from civilised life. When I was down at the Grahams' in the spring, they said you were coming down there, and then at the last moment cried off. We were all quite disappointed. What is taking you to India now? Going to preach the doctrine of social and intellectual equality to the Hindu women and incite them to revolt? Marry some old Buddhist Priest, build a little cottage on the top of the Himalayas and live there, discuss philosophy and meditate? I believe that's what you'd like. I really shouldn't wonder if I heard you'd done it!"

She laughed and took out her cigarette case.

She smoked slowly.

"I've been here a long time, four years, and I want change. I was glad to see how well you succeeded in that election," she said. "You were much interested in it, were you not?"

"Oh, yes. We had a stiff fight. It tells in my favour, you know, though it was not exactly a personal matter. But it was a great worry."

"Don't you think," she said, "you were wrong in sending that letter to the papers? It would have strengthened your position to have remained silent."

"Yes, perhaps so; I think so now, but I did it under advice. However, we've won, so it's all right." He leaned back in the chair.

"Are you pretty fit?"

"Oh, yes; pretty well; bored, you know. One doesn't know what all this working and striving is for sometimes."

"Where are you going for your holiday this year?"

"Oh, Scotland, I suppose; I always do; the old quarters."

"Why don't you go to Norway? It would be more change for you and rest you more. Did you get a book on sport in Norway?"

"Did you send it me? How kind of you! I read it with much interest. I was almost inclined to start off there and then. I suppose it is the kind of *vis inertiæ* that creeps over one as one grows older that sends one back to the old place. A change would be much better."

"There's a list at the end of the book" she said, "of exactly the things one needs to take. I thought it would save trouble; you could just give it to your man, and let him get them all. Have you still got him?"

"Oh, yes. He's as faithful to me as a dog. I think nothing would induce him to leave me. He won't allow me to go out hunting since I sprained my foot last autumn. I have to do it surreptitiously. He thinks I can't keep my seat with a sprained ankle; but he's a very good fellow; takes care of me like a mother." He smoked quietly with the firelight glowing on his black coat. "But what are you going to India for? Do you know anyone there?"

"No," she said. "I think it will be so splendid. I've always been a great deal interested in the East. It's a complex, interesting life."

He turned and looked at her.

"Going to seek for more experience, you'll say, I suppose. I never knew a woman throw herself away as you do; a woman with your brilliant parts and attractions, to let the whole of life slip through your hands, and make nothing of it. You ought to be the most successful woman in London. Oh, yes; I know what you are going to say: 'You don't care.' That's just it; you don't. You are always going to get experience, going to get everything, and you never do. You are always going to write when you know enough, and you are never satisfied that you do. You ought to be making your two thousand a year, but you don't care. That's just it! Living, burying yourself here with a lot of old frumps. You will never do anything. You could have everything and you let it slip."

"Oh, my life is very full," she said. "There are only two things that are absolute realities, love and knowledge, and you can't escape them."

She had thrown her cigarette end away and was looking into the fire, smiling.

"I've let these rooms to a woman friend of mine." She glanced round the room, smiling. "She doesn't know I'm going to leave these things here for her. She'll like them because they were mine. The world's very beautiful, I think—delicious."

"Oh, yes. But what do you do with it? What do you make of it? You ought to settle down and marry like other women, not go wandering about the world to India and China and Italy, and God knows where. You are simply making a mess of your life. You're always surrounding yourself with all sorts of extraordinary people. If I hear any man or woman is a great friend of yours, I always say: 'What's the matter? Lost his money? Lost his character? Got an incurable disease?' I believe the only way in which anyone becomes interesting to you is by having some complaint of mind or body. I believe you worship rags. To come and shut yourself up in a place like this away from everybody and everything! It's a mistake; it's idiotic, you know."

"I'm very happy," she said. "You see," she said, leaning forwards towards the fire with her hands on her knees, "what matters is that something should need you. It isn't a question of love. What's the use of being near a thing if other people could serve it as well as you can. If they could serve it better, it's pure selfishness. It's the need of one thing for another that makes the organic bond of union. You love mountains and horses, but they don't need you; so what's the use of saying anything about it! I suppose the most absolutely delicious thing in life is to feel a thing needs you, and to give at the moment it needs. Things that don't need you, you must love from a distance."

"Oh, but a woman like you ought to marry, ought to have children. You go squandering yourself on every old beggar or forlorn female or escaped criminal you meet; it may be very nice for them, but it's a mistake from your point of view."

He touched the ash gently with the tip of his little finger and let it fall.

"I intend to marry. It's a curious thing," he said, resuming his pose with an elbow on one knee and his head bent forward on one side, so that she saw the brown hair with its close curls a little tinged with grey at the sides, "that when a man reaches a certain age he wants to marry. He doesn't fall in love; it's not that he definitely plans anything; but he has a feeling that he ought to have a home and a wife and children. I suppose it is the same kind of feeling that makes a bird build nests at certain times of the year. It's not love; it's something else. When I was a young man I used to despise men for getting married; wondered what they did it for; they had everything to lose and nothing to gain. But when a man gets to be six-and-thirty his feeling changes. It's not love, passion, he wants; it's a home; it's a wife and children. He may have a house and servants; it isn't the same thing. I should have thought a woman would have felt it too."

She was quiet for a minute, holding a cigarette between her fingers; then she said slowly:

"Yes, at times a woman has a curious longing to have a child, especially when she gets near to thirty or over it. It's something distinct from love for any definite person. But it's a thing one has to get over. For a woman, marriage is much more serious than for a man. She might pass her life without meeting a man whom she could possibly love, and, if she met him, it might not be right or possible. Marriage has become very complex now it has become so largely intellectual. Won't you have another?"

She held out the case to him. "You can light it from mine." She bent forward for him to light it.

"You are a man who ought to marry. You've no absorbing mental work with which the woman would interfere; it would complete you." She sat back, smoking serenely.

"Yes," he said, "but life is too busy; I never find time to look for one, and I haven't a fancy for the pink-and-white prettiness so common and that some men like so. I need something else. If I am to have a wife I shall have to go to America to look for one."

"Yes, an American would suit you best."

"Yes," he said, "I don't want a woman to look after; she must be self-sustaining and she mustn't bore you. You know what I mean. Life is too full of cares to have a helpless child added to them."

"Yes," she said, standing up and leaning with her elbow against the fireplace. "The kind of woman you want would be young and strong; she need not be excessively beautiful, but she must be attractive; she must have energy, but not too strongly marked an individuality; she must be largely neutral; she need not give you too passionate or too deep a devotion, but she must second you in a thoroughly rational manner. She must have the same aims and tastes that you have. No woman has the right to marry a man if she has to bend herself out of shape for him. She might wish to, but she could never be to him with all her passionate endeavour what the other woman could be to him without trying. Character will dominate over all and will come out at last."

She looked down into the fire.

"When you marry you mustn't marry a woman who flatters you too much. It is always a sign of falseness somewhere. If a woman absolutely loves you as herself, she will criticise and understand you as herself. Two people who are to live through life together must be able to look into each other's eyes and speak the truth. That helps one through life. You would find many such women in America," she said: "women who would help you to succeed, who would not drag you down."

"Yes, that's my idea. But how am I to obtain the ideal woman?"

"Go and look for her. Go to America instead of Scotland this year. It is perfectly right. A man has a right to look for what he needs. With a woman it is different. That's one of the radical differences between men and women."

She looked downwards into the fire.

"It's a law of her nature and of sex relationship.' There's nothing arbitrary or conventional about it any more than there is in her having to bear her child while the male does not. Intellectually we may both be alike. I suppose if fifty men and fifty women had to solve a mathematical problem, they would all do it in the same way; the more abstract and intellectual, the more alike we are. The nearer you approach to the personal and sexual, the more different we are. If I were to represent men's and women's natures," she said, "by a diagram, I would take two circular discs; the right side of each I should paint bright red; then I would shade the red away till in a spot on the left edge it became blue in the one and green in the other. That spot represents sex, and the nearer you come to it, the more the two discs differ in colour. Well then, if you turn them so that the red sides touch, they seem to be exactly alike, but if you turn them so that the green and blue paint form their point of contact, they will seem to be entirely unlike. That's why you notice the brutal, sensual men invariably believe women are entirely different from men, another species of creature; and very cultured, intellectual men sometimes believe we are exactly alike. You see, sex love in its substance may be the same in both of us; in the form of its expression it must differ. It is not man's fault; it is nature's. If a man loves a woman, he has a right to try to make her love him because he can do it openly, directly, without bending. There need be no subtlety, no indirectness. With a woman it's not so; she can take no love that is not laid openly, simply, at her feet. Nature ordains that she should never show what she feels; the woman who had told a man she loved him would have put between them a barrier once and for ever that could not be crossed; and if she subtly drew him towards her, using the woman's means—silence, finesse, the dropped handkerchief, the surprise visit, the gentle assertion she had not thought to see him when she had come a long way to meet him, then she would be damned; she would hold the love, but she would have desecrated it by subtlety; it would have no value. Therefore she must always go with her arms folded sexually; only the love which lays itself down at her feet and implores of her to accept it is love she can ever rightly take up. That is the true difference between a man and a woman. You may seek for love because you can do it openly; we cannot because we must do it subtly. A woman should always walk with her arms folded. Of course friendship is different. You are on a perfect equality with man then; you can ask him to come and see you as I asked you. That's the beauty of the intellect and intellectual life to a woman, that she drops her shackles a little; and that is why she shrinks from sex so. If she were dying perhaps, or doing something equal to death, she might .... Death means so much more to a woman than a man; when you knew you were dying, to look round on the world and feel the bond of sex that has broken and crushed you all your life gone, nothing but the human left, no woman any more, to meet everything on perfectly even ground. There's no reason why you shouldn't go to America and look for a wife perfectly deliberately. You will have to tell no lies. Look till you find a woman that you absolutely love, that you have not the smallest doubt suits you apart from love, and then ask her to marry you. You must have children; the life of an old childless man is very sad."

"Yes, I should like to have children. I often feel now, what is it all for, this work, this striving, and no one to leave it to? It's a blank, suppose I succeed ...?"

"Suppose you get your title?"

"Yes; what is it all worth to me if I've no one to leave it to? That's my feeling. It's really very strange to be sitting and talking like this to you. But you are so different from other women. If all women were like you, all your theories of the equality of men and women would work. You're the only woman with whom I never realise that she is a woman."

"Yes," she said.

She stood looking down into the fire.

"How long will you stay in India?"

"Oh, I'm not coming back."

"Not coming back! That's impossible. You will be breaking the hearts of half the people here if you don't. I never knew a woman who had such power of entrapping men's hearts as you have in spite of that philosophy of yours. I don't know," he smiled, "that I should not have fallen into the snare myself— three years ago I almost thought I should—if you hadn't always attacked me so incontinently and persistently on all and every point and on each and every occasion. A man doesn't like pain. A succession of slaps damps him. But it doesn't seem to have that effect on other men .... There was that fellow down in the country when I was there last year, perfectly ridiculous. You know his name..." He moved his fingers to try and remember it— "big, yellow moustache, a major, gone to the east coast of Africa now; the ladies unearthed it that he was always carrying about a photograph of yours in his pocket; and he used to take out little scraps of things you printed and show them to people mysteriously. He almost had a duel with a man one night after dinner because he mentioned you; he seemed to think there was something incongruous between your name and—"

"I do not like to talk of any man who has loved me," she said. "However small and poor his nature may be, he has given me his best. There is nothing ridiculous in love. I think a woman should feel that all the love men have given her which she has not been able to return is a kind of crown set up above her which she is always trying to grow tall enough to wear. I can't bear to think that all the love that has been given me has been wasted on something unworthy of it. Men have been very beautiful and greatly honoured me. I am grateful to them. If a man tells you he loves you," she said, looking into the fire, "with his breast uncovered before you for you to strike him if you will, the least you can do is to put out your hand and cover it up from other people's eyes. If I were a deer," she said, "and a stag got hurt following me, even though I could not have him for a companion, I would stand still and scrape the sand with my foot over the place where his blood had fallen; the rest of the herd should never know he had been hurt there following me. I would cover the blood up, if I were a deer," she said, and then she was silent.

Presently she sat down in her chair and said, with her hand before her: "Yet, you know, I have not the ordinary feeling about love. I think the one who is loved confers the benefit on the one who loves, it's been so great and beautiful that it should be loved. I think the man should be grateful to the woman or the woman to the man whom they have been able to love, whether they have been loved back or whether circumstances have divided them or not." She stroked her knee softly with her hand.

"Well, really, I must go now." He pulled out his watch. "It's so fascinating sitting here talking that I could stay all night, but I've still two engagements." He rose; she rose also and stood before him looking up at him for a moment.

"How well you look! I think you have found the secret of perpetual youth. You don't look a day older than when I first saw you just four years ago. You always look as if you were on fire and being burnt up, but you never are, you know."

He looked down at her with a kind of amused face as one does at an interesting child or a big Newfoundland dog.

"When shall we see you back?"

"Oh, not at all!"

"Not at all! Oh, we must have you back; you belong here, you know. You'll get tired of your Buddhist and come back to us."

"You didn't mind my asking you to come and say good-bye?" she said in a childish manner unlike her determinateness when she discussed anything impersonal. "I wanted to say good-bye to everyone. If one hasn't said good-bye one feels restless and feels one would have to come back. If one has said goodbye to all one's friends, then one knows it is all ended."

"Oh, this isn't a final farewell! You must come in ten years' time and we'll compare notes—you about your Buddhist Priest, I about my fair ideal American; and we'll see who succeeded best."

She laughed.

"I shall always see your movements chronicled in the newspapers, so we shall not be quite sundered; and you will hear of me perhaps."

"Yes, I hope you will be very successful."

She was looking at him, with her eyes wide open, from head to foot. He turned to the chair where his coat hung.

"Can't I help you put it on?"

"Oh, no, thank you."

He put it on.

"Button the throat," she said, "the room is warm."

He turned to her in his great-coat and with his gloves. They were standing near the door.

"Well, good-bye. I hope you will have a very pleasant time."

He stood looking down upon her, wrapped in his great-coat.

She put up one hand a little in the air. "I want to ask you something," she said quickly.

"Well, what is it?"

"Will you please kiss me?"

For a moment he looked down at her, then he bent over her.

In after years he could never tell certainly, but he always thought she put up her hand and rested it on the crown of his head, with a curious soft caress, something like a mother's touch when her child is asleep and she does not want to wake it. Then he looked round, and she was gone. The door had closed noiselessly. For a moment he stood motionless, then he walked to the fireplace and looked down into the fender at a little cigarette end lying there, then he walked quickly back to the door and opened it. The stairs were in darkness and silence. He rang the bell violently. The old woman came up. He asked her where the lady was. She said she had gone out, she had a cab waiting. He asked when she would be back. The old woman said, "Not at all"; she had left. He asked where she had gone. The woman said she did not know; she had left orders that all her letters should be kept for six or eight months till she wrote and sent her address. He asked whether she had no idea where he might find her. The woman said no. He walked up to a space in the wall where a picture had hung and stood staring at it as though the picture were still hanging there. He drew his mouth as though he were emitting a long whistle, but no sound came. He gave the old woman ten shillings and went downstairs.

   That was eight years ago.

   How beautiful life must have been to it that it looks so young still!

# On the Banks of a Full River

It was in the year 18—, the year of the great rains.

I, a young girl of sixteen, was going home from the South where I had been at school.

We travelled in a Cobb & Co.'s coach, nine passengers inside and four out; and all day and night it rained. We did in two days the journey we should have done in one; and when they changed horses they gave us no time to sleep. Night and day we travelled. On the evening of the ninth day we stopped on the banks of a full river. The greasy, coffee-coloured water flowed level with the banks, and the heads of half-drowned willow trees showed themselves on either side. We should not be able to cross that night, it might be not for days.

We looked out through the pouring rain. Beside us was a little mud house, the only habitation within thirty miles. It was square, with a divided door and one small window. The man to whom it belonged came out to meet us; he lived there alone and sold liquor to the passers-by. It was arranged between him and the driver we should stay there for the night. We alighted from the coach and streamed into the house; we found it consisted of one small room. I and the woman who was my only female travelling companion stood before the fire drying our clothes which had got damp in the passage from the coach to the house; the men stood round the table drinking bad brandy and whisky in cups and glasses, while the driver went out to see to his horses. There was nothing to be had to eat but some stale biscuits from a tin and some leathery roaster-cake. Some one brought up the one chair the room contained and an empty soap box, and the woman and I sat down before the fire. By and by the driver came in, and the night darkened down quickly. The men still stood smoking and drinking round the table. The rain was falling less heavily. After a while the men conferred together and they decided, with that gentleness which rough men travelling alone with women always show, that they should all find shelter in the coach and the hut be left to us alone. The owner put the large stump of an uprooted willow tree upon the fire and in half an hour the men stumbled out; we could hear them swearing and grumbling in the rain on the way to the coach; and for an hour we caught broken peals of ribald laughter or obscene songs through the sound of the falling rain; then gradually all became quiet.

The room in which they left us had a bare mud floor on which was only a white sheepskin that lay before the fire; on the brown mud wall there was a rack with two guns and a pistol, and in the centre of the room stood the table with empty bottles and glasses, and in the corner was a stretcher with one band broken and a thin mattress and three dirty blankets. There was no place in which one might lie down. The firelight flickered over the walls; the three inches of tallow candle they had left in a black bottle on the table had burnt itself out.

I grew tired of sitting on the soap box and slipped down and crouched on the white sheepskin before the fire. The woman sat in the chair on the right, her head so far back that the firelight did not shine on it. One could hardly tell whether she was awake or asleep.

She was a tall, slight woman dressed in black, and might have been any age between thirty and forty-five. She had been very kind to me all the way; in the night when, without my knowing it, I grew sleepy and my head dropped, she laid it on her shoulder and I woke with it there in the morning. When it was cold she made me put on her great fur cloak, such as women from England have, and we talked of the scenery we passed through and of books, and we were friends, though neither of us had asked any question or knew anything of the other.

The rain still fell heavily, and far off one could hear the rush of the river. I stared into the fire till the blaze from the glowing coals almost scorched my eyelashes.

Suddenly I turned to my companion. "Life is very wicked; it is very unjust," I said.

I raised myself on my knees.

She looked down at me and leaned forward. She had seemed almost asleep. She did not speak.

"It is very cruel; it is very unjust!" I said. "It is no use trying! Some people have everything and some people have nothing; and things are not as they should be!"

She put out her hand and I felt it on my head for a moment. Then she drew it back.

I was young, and I was suffering my first surprise at my first shattered ideal.

The woman raised herself and looked down at me. I laid my clenched fists upon my knees.

"I have found no balancing interrelation between the material and mental world," she said. "If you go with love in your heart to fetch a cup of water for your friend, there is no relation between the intensity of the love and the cup's fracture; if that is what you mean by justice in life, then there is none. But, in the emotional and intellectual spheres, human nature has a deep power of working out compensations; what is taken from us on the one hand works itself back to us on the other. There is nothing mysterious in this, just as there is nothing mysterious in one scale of a balance going down and another up when you move matter from one to the other, though it might seem so to a little baby. There are times, thinking over life," she said, "I have almost seemed to see the terms in which this balancing process might be stated so as to be clearly grasped intellectually. I think it is there."

I sat looking into the fire. My heart was very bitter. I had had my first ideal shattered, my great plan for what was beautiful broken. I was beating my wings against the bars of the inevitable in life as young things do, battering the wings but not hurting the bars.

"Yes, but you do not know," I said. And after a while I told her my story. It was a long story, and seemed to me then the only one in the world. There is no need I should repeat it fully:

Three years before I had gone to school on a farm in the South; it was a mixed school where boys and girls were taught together. There was one boy three years older than I. He and I were always at the head of the school. He worked hard at first to get up to me because he could not bear a girl should stand higher; but afterwards we became great friends.

> (*Note by S.C.C.S.*—There is evidently a page or so missing here; the narrative would introduce the other girl and begin the delineation of her character in her attitude towards the lad; the delineation is, however, clear enough in the passages immediately following. Apparently they had been having, were having, school holidays when the tale continues.)

... taught him to make flutes of reeds; sometimes she sat in the fork of the apple trees and he lay below and she threw down fruit to him; sometimes she brought her books to him and asked him questions, and she said he was so wonderful when he could explain; and the one thing he had never needed was praise. Then the holidays came to an end. We had brought much work to do that he might pass the last examination; but, when I came to look for him, he was walking laughing with her, and I hid the books under my arm. The last day of the holidays she came to me and said he was not going back to school. Her father had offered him £20 a month to oversee the wine farming. They could have got anyone else for five, she said, but her father had done it because she asked him. "All this is mine," she said. "There is no one else to inherit it; my father lets me do what I like with it and I want him to have it." I talked with him once. He seemed a little sorry, but he could not refuse £20. I did not go back to school for the next quarter; I came straight home; I was on my journey up. I sat beside the fire and told the story.

"You see," I said, when I had finished it, "he is lost, his beautiful possibilities are dead; she will drag him down, down. It would have been better if she had killed him!" And I laid my clenched hands on my knees. It would have been easy for me to have killed myself, I so hated that girl as I stood there.

The woman said: "Are you quite just? Are you sure it is she who has dragged him down?"

"I hate her, oh, I hate her so!" I said. "I would have forgiven her if she had killed him, but not for this."

(*Note by S.C.C.S.*—A gap occurs here.)

"... study more. You see," I said, "I don't mind that he hates me, but I mind that he will never do anything more; he will marry and settle down. She has killed him. It is as if she were a soft greasy snake, and she had crept over him, and put her tooth into his body and the poison has crept in and in and he is dead, he is asleep for ever."

She said: "Can other people ever poison us?"

I said: "They can! But I could wake him. That is the terrible thing. If I could tell him what she was, if I could have had one half-hour's talk with him (and he had sought it), I could make him fling her off as a man flings off a toad when he wakes and sees it sitting on him. That's the terrible thing! That's why I've asked my friends to get me home at once because I dare not stay there. If once I were to talk against her to him, then my soul would be lost, as hers is now. You see I can't," I said. "I must go away where I can never see him any more and leave him to her!"

I looked up, but the woman was sitting motionless on the chair and the firelight was dancing on the guns in the rack.

"You see," I said, "people say she is a clever woman; she is strong; they say she can have everything; it's the poor, weak, gentle, little women that need looking after, that must be taken care of. It's a lie; it's we that are weak! If the snake once thinks it wrong to use its poison fangs and begins to develop feet, and makes a noise with them as it comes on, is it stronger? It's higher, of course, higher! What is that *higher*? It is weakness. Is there anything so strong as the snake when it creeps on noiselessly with its fangs and its silent glide? The horse, the elephant, the lion, are nothing to it. Take this from it and what has it left? It has not the speed, the claws, the thick skin of the others! A snake without its poison bag, who gives notice when it is coming," I laughed,— "every creature can put his foot on its head and crush out its poor unused poison bag that it has never used. It will never be a lion or an elephant for all its feet. A woman with intellect and strength and the ideal of acting strictly by other women—haugh! She is dirt beneath everyone's feet. There is nothing so weak on the earth. She will never be a man! Life gave women subtlety and lying and meanness and flattery that they might defend themselves. They have all things if they will use their tools."

We were silent for a moment; then she said: "Do you think any strong, intellectual woman ever really wanted to be a weak one? Is it not better to have half-developed hands and feet, and be trodden on? Does it matter so much what one has as what one is?"

And she said after a time: "Does one really ever gain anything by subtlety? Is it not seeming?"

I said: "Oh, it is such a terrible thing to be a woman. You can do nothing for those you love. You must wait, crush out, kill, in yourself. The old passive women who took indirect means, they are happy."

She said: "Do you think so?"

Then she said after a time: "I knew two women in England; one was older, and the younger lived with her; she was her cousin. The younger was what the world calls a strong, intellectual woman; she painted. The other was what the world calls a gentle, womanly woman; she had married, when she was young, a rich man, and had three children. She had a very beautiful home, and she always pictured herself to herself as the central image in it, the most beautiful of all. The younger woman knew an artist who worked at the same studio; she loved him as only people can love who love the work and the objects of others, not only their persons. Every day she went to his studio and criticised his work; when he was satisfied, she was not; she wanted something better; she had a greater dream for his future than she ever told him. They were very near to each other. She never spoke of love to him: what need is there to talk of love to a man, when he knows his work is more to you than your own; and you love your own?"

"And then?" I said.

"After two years he came to the house where she lived with her older cousin. At first the woman took little notice of him; then she used to have glasses of jelly ready for him when he came, and let him lie on the sofa in her great room in the garden. He took her to his studio: she stood still a long time before one picture, and said, 'Oh, please don't speak to me; it makes me feel like a beautiful summer's day to look at it'; and the young woman had told him to burn it; it was unworthy of him. She said she wanted her picture painted with her little baby, and he painted her as a madonna with her child in her arms with their cheeks touching. I do not think he cared for her then. He simply painted her. She gave the picture to her husband, and asked the young man to come to her house oftener."

"And then?"

"Then one day she talked of him to the younger woman. I do not say she told the younger woman she loved him; that would have been wrong in a married woman; but she knew the nature of the younger woman; she spoke so that she implied that she liked him. When she wanted to go for a drive she did not say to the younger woman, 'You stay at home. I want to go this afternoon.' She said, 'You go, dear, I don't mind staying at all; I'm sure you'll enjoy it more than I do'; and then the younger woman stayed. And that night it was moonlight and the younger woman was walking in agony on a terrace that ran beside the house. It was terrible another woman should love the man she loved; in a moment all the lovely beauty was gone ..."

I said, "I hate that woman!"

... "and then the older woman and the man came out and stood under a great tree to hear the nightingales sing, and she talked of the younger woman, and the young man said, 'Yes, she is too restlessly energetic,' and so they talked. The elder knew that the younger was there, and the younger knew she knew it. Then she went into the house. You see her love was broken. She thought what was best to be done. You can't cope with such women, you can't touch them, you must leave them. The day you touch them you sink to their level; you don't only lose your love, you degrade it: it was white as far as she was concerned. So she thought the thing out; and that night she packed her things; the next day she left. She did not say good-bye to the man. She came out to Africa; for many years she lived here. After a while, seven or eight years, she married a man who was dying of consumption and took care of his two children when he was dead. She had a happy life. It was nice to take care of the children. She had plenty to do."

The woman sat still.

"And the other woman?" I asked.

"She lived on in her beautiful house with her husband and children and was very happy. The young artist never understood why his friend left; he came often to the house; and lay on the great sofa, and the woman gave him jelly and soups to strengthen him for his work. He never worked much, but he always came to see her; they were very intimate friends till her husband died,"

>(*Note by S.C.C.S.*—The page numbered 16 by Olive ends here; what follows is on page numbered 18.)

"... Need you envy a man for holding dust in his hand? What is the use of possessing a man if you hold him and possess him through flattery? Is a man worth having who desires it?"

I said, "Yes, but she had what she desired. When her husband died she could have him always with her; the last little restraint was gone; she could wait on him and help him. That is what we women want when we love a man."

She sat still, twirling the ...

>(*Note by S.C.C.S.*—Here ends page 18. What follows is on page numbered 20 by Olive.)

I said, "What?"

She said, "Pity her, she married him."

We sat still in the firelight.

I said at last: "Did those two women ever meet again?"

She said: "Yes, once, after years. The elder woman came out to South Africa and they met once."

I sat looking into the fire. I and the Stepmother

# The Wax Doll and the Stepmother

Rolly was a small boy five years old who wore knickerbockers. He had great brown eyes and curls that hung over his forehead; but Nina, his sister, who was a year older, had yellow hair and a white face. She was so thin that when Rolly tried hard he could lift her off the ground.

They had no mother, but their Papa was kind to them, and one day when he came from town he brought a beautiful wax doll for Nina. She had many dolls, but none like this one. Its hair was real; you could curl and comb it as much as you pleased; it had real eyelashes, and fingers and toes of wax, and the best of all was it had little teeth. You could see them always, for its mouth was never shut.

Nurse Bromage, who looked after the children, said it was quite too good to play with, and put the doll away on the top shelf. Nina cried; she loved the doll so much, with its little teeth. But Nurse Bromage did not care; for, you see, she was a cross old thing and didn't mind if other people weren't happy, if only she was. But sometimes she went to visit her cousin in the country, and then Jennie the housemaid used to let them play with it as much as they pleased. One day when they were playing with her one of the tucks in the doll's flannel petticoat got loosened. Nina kissed her and Rolly told her they didn't mean to do it; and so they thought it was all right.

A little time after that Nurse Bromage told them that when their Papa came home the next day he was going to bring them a new Mamma. The children clapped their hands when they heard that.

"Then we will have a Mamma too!" they said, "like the other children!"

"Yes," said Nina. "Perhaps she will come and kiss us when we are in bed, like the pretty lady kisses the little girl in the picture in Papa's bedroom!"

But Nurse Bromage knit up her forehead and shook her head.

"All the house will belong to your new Mamma," she said, "and all the things in it. She will not like you at all, because if it were not for you she would get all your Papa's things when he dies; but now you will have to get some."

Then Nina and Rolly were quite unhappy. They went and sat on a little box behind the door where they always sat when Nurse Bromage scolded them.

"We'll tell the new Mamma that we don't want any of Papa's things," said Nina. "Won't we, Rolly?"

"We'll tell her just as soon as she comes," said Rolly. "But perhaps she looks like Nurse Bromage!"

"Oh dear!" said Nina, and hung her head. Her neck was so thin that when she hung it, it always seemed as though it might break off.

The next day when the carriage came the servants and the two children went into the great hall to meet their Papa and the lady. Nina had on a white dress with a blue sash; and Rolly had a black velvet suit with three pockets, one in the jacket and two in the trousers.

"I think she'll think I'm quite a big boy, when she sees me in this," said Rolly.

When the carriage stopped their Papa helped out the lady. She was very beautiful; tall, with red cheeks, and lips like cherries, and black hair shining like a crow's wing. She had on a silk dress with a black rustling train, and that made her grander still. She was very beautiful, but she had not a happy face. No one had ever taught her that it was not money and fine houses and fine clothes that could make a person happy; and so her heart felt all over as though it were pricked by little pins. So the hearts of all people feel, when they want more than they have got and are not full of love.

"She isn't like Nurse Bromage. She's just like your best wax-doll," Rolly whispered; but Nina was so afraid she did not lift her face.

When their new Mamma came into the hall, "These are my little children," the Papa said. But she did not look at them; she only bent down and touched Rolly's forehead with her lips. Nina she did not kiss at all.

"Rolly, I can't tell her she can have all Papa's things! Oh! I am so afraid of her," said Nina, when they went up the long stairs holding each other's hands.

"*I'm* not frightened," said Rolly, "*I'm* a *man* and you are only a woman, you know. But I don't like her. Why didn't she kiss you?"

"Oh, Rolly, I love her!" said Nina, with tears in her eyes.

That evening Nurse Bromage brought them to sit in the parlour for a little while. Their Papa gave them some nuts to crack, but the beautiful lady never spoke to them; she sat with her screen before the fire.

"You see, Nina," said Rolly, when they were lying in their little beds in the dark, "it is quite true; she does hate us. And I don't love her; not a bit. I'd like to take my big drum and beat it at her bedroom door when she's asleep!"

"Oh, you mustn't say so, Rolly!" said Nina.

But Rolly didn't care, and soon went to sleep and so did she. But the cough soon woke her up again, and she lay alone in the dark, and a beautiful thought came to her. She wished it would be morning soon that she might tell Rolly. She folded her little hands together, and pressed the palms. For all that she couldn't tell him when the morning came, for Nurse Bromage was by, and no one could say anything nice while *she* was there. After breakfast she taught them their letters. When Nina called B, D, she whipped her hands with a little rod tied with a red string; but she didn't whip Rolly because he was her favourite.

By and by, when it was afternoon, Nurse Bromage went to sleep on the sofa. Then Nina called Rolly behind the door.

"What is it?" said Rolly, coming close and lifting his ear.

"You know my wax doll, Rolly; my best wax doll?" said Nina.

"Yes," said Rolly.

"I want to give it to her, Rolly. Do you think she'll like it?"

"Who?"

"Our new Mamma."

"Oh, yes!" said Rolly, "of course she will. I don't believe she ever saw one like it in her life before!"

"And you'll take it to her, Rolly? You are not afraid, are you?"

"I should think not," said Rolly, sticking his hands into his knickerbocker pockets, and swelling himself out. "I'll take it."

"Let us go and fetch it before Nurse wakes," said Nina. But Rolly paused, shaking his head and looking very sagacious.

"She'll find out and she'll whip you, Nina!"

"It doesn't matter," said Nina, a little sorrowfully. "You know she will whatever I do."

So they went to the next room. Rolly pulled the chair, and Nina put the footstool on; and he climbed up, while she held fast. When he had got the doll he came down quickly; and they took a beautiful piece of white paper with a silver edge, that came with the china tea-service, to wrap it in.

"Isn't she lovely?" said Nina, as she laid it in the paper and smoothed out the little soft curls.

"She just is!" said Rolly. "Aren't you sorry to give her away?"

"No," said Nina; but when she looked at the little teeth her lip trembled. She gave it to Rolly to hold while she went for a piece of string. They neither of them knew how to tie a bow; but Rolly said he didn't think it mattered, because their new Mamma could untie a knot by herself, he guessed.

"You must tell her I'm sorry the one tuck is out," said Nina, "and I would have mended it only I don't know how to work."

Rolly put the doll under his arm, and Nina went with him to the door of the long passage.

"You are not afraid, are you?"

"Oh, no!" said Rolly; but his heart beat so that the doll against his breast went up and down, up and down.

He walked up the long passage to the door of the new Mamma's bedroom. He gave a little knock with his forefinger, but no one answered. He thought there could be no one inside, so gave a very brave one with his fist.

The new Mamma said, "Who is there?"

"I," said Rolly; and he pushed open the door, and walked in.

It was almost dinner-time, and there were going to be visitors that evening. The lady was sitting before the glass dressing. She had on a black velvet dress, and the sleeves were wide open to show her arms, as white as the snow, and covered with bracelets.

Rolly walked in and stood before her looking at her.

"What do you want?" she asked.

He was such a wee boy when he stood so close beside her, and she was a grand, beautiful woman.

"I've brought this for you," said Rolly, "and you may keep it for your own. It's Nina sends it to you."

He put the parcel down in her lap, and folded his hands behind him.

"And who is Nina?" asked the lady.

"Why, Nina *is* Nina, to be sure! My sister," said Rolly. "And she says you mustn't mind the one tuck being out, because she would have mended it if she could."

The lady unrolled the parcel and looked at the doll.

"You see," he said, picking up the doll's dress and showing the petticoat, "that's the tuck; but it's all that's the matter with her. Isn't it lovely?" said Rolly, sticking his hands in his pockets and watching to see what effect it would have upon her.

"You didn't notice the teeth, I suppose, did you?" said Rolly, eyeing her critically. "It's real teeth, and the hair too. You can put oil on if you like."

"Who told Nina to send it?" asked the lady.

"Why, no one," said Rolly; "she thought of it last night when she was in bed."

"What made her want to send it to me?"

"Well," said Rolly, drawing confidentially nearer, "you mustn't tell, of course; but Nina, she said if she gave it you, perhaps you'd kiss her, like the lady in the picture kisses the little girl, you know, when she's in bed."

The lady looked down at the doll. "Go and tell Nina, that I say 'thank you.'"

"It's a beautiful doll," said Rolly, fearing she had not enough admired it, "and the boots are red. Good-bye!"

When he got to the door he looked back. "I'll tell her you don't mind about the petticoat, eh?"

"Yes," said the lady, so Rolly went.

That evening the children sat on their hassocks before the fire. Nurse Bromage had taken the light out and gone downstairs to get some of the nice things that were over from the big people's dinner; so they drew their little hassocks as close together as they could and sat looking at the fire.

"She said 'thank you,'" said Rolly; "she must have liked it!"

"Oh no, I think she's angry," said Nina.

Rolly could see two large tears on her face, so he rubbed her cheeks with his coat sleeve. It was rather rough, but it did her good.

"I don't believe she could be so bad as not to like your doll," he said; and they sat still looking at the fire.

Then the door opened softly.

"There she comes!" said Rolly, looking round—"I knew she would."

But the little girl sat quite huddled up with fear, and quite cold. The lady came in; you could see in the firelight how beautiful she was, with her diamonds sparkling, and her velvet dress and her black hair.

"This is Nina!" said Rolly. "Here she sits!"

The lady did not speak. She brought the rocking-chair from the corner and put it before the fire and sat down.

"Come!" she said; and she lifted the little girl up with her strong white hands and sat her on her knee. She held the thin little face fast and kissed the mouth six times, very softly.

"My dear little daughter," she said, and laid the head down on her breast.

Rolly, on his hassock before the fire, stroked his little knees for gladness, and his round eyes were just as bright as the coals.

The new Mamma called him to come and stand at her side. She put her arm quite tight round him.

"You are just like the wax doll, and much prettier too," he said, looking up at her. "Nina and I, we like you very much. But I didn't like you first."

"Why not?"

"Because—a—because—a—because—you didn't kiss her. But I like you now," he said, edging suddenly nearer to her, and taking hold of her face with one hand to turn it to him. "And you know, New Mamma, we didn't want *any* of Papa's things. You can have them all. *I'll* take care of Nina," he added, drawing himself up; "I'm nearly a big man already. I can climb into bed right from the ground by myself, and button my clothes too!"

"You dear little boy!" said the lady, and she kissed him on his eyes, and on his forehead, and on the brown curls that hung down.

Then Rolly put his head down on her shoulder, and rubbed his curls softly against her neck.

"It's so nice and happy; just like a birthday! Isn't it, Nina?" he said.

But Nina only pressed the lady's waist with all her little strength.

"And you won't let Nurse Bromage s-col-d Nina for giving you her doll; will you, my New Mamma?" said Rolly. "Poor Nina, you know!"

"No one shall hurt her now," said the lady, "she is my little daughter."

"Yes; and I'll be your big son too, if you like!" said Rolly, looking up, "and take care of you!"

"So you shall, my darling."

"Yes," said Rolly, very much excited, "and—I—I'll always get you—canary seed—for your bird—and—I—I'll build you a house of shells—and—and—"

"You shall do it all for me, just to-morrow," said the lady. "Where are your little beds? I shall carry Nina, and you shall show me. I want to undress you both."

"Will you kiss us when we have our nightgowns on?"

"Yes."

Rolly put his mouth close to her ear.

"Will you lie with us a little while?"

"Yes."
"Close?"
"Yes."
"Oh! it's just like a birthday," said Rolly—"only it's much nicer!"

# The Adventures of Master Towser

### I—His Sorrow

Small Towser sat with his tail in a puddle of mud. The puddle was small, but so was his tail. His nose was turned down to the paving-stones; there were two drops running down towards the tip of it, but they weren't raindrops, though the afternoon was sad and cloudy enough—they came from his eyes. Presently, out of the swell gate of the house over the way came a most respectable-looking dog, of a very comfortable appearance, and as big as eight Towsers, for he was a mastiff.

"Why don't you take your tail out of the puddle?" asked the comfortable-looking dog.

Towser gave it a feeble little splutter in the mud: he didn't know why he let it hang there, except that he was miserable.

"Starve you over at your house?" inquired the comfortable dog.

"No," said Towser, "there are dishes of bones and nice little bits of fat in the kitchen."

"Other dogs bite you?"

"No." Towser shook his head.

"Have to sleep out in the cold?"

"No, I've got a house," said Towser.

"You're a nice gentlemanly-looking little dog; you oughtn't to be unhappy. What's the matter?" asked the comfortable-looking dog.

"I'm not any good," said Towser.

The big dog didn't comprehend.

"I want someone to love me," said Towser; "I want to help somebody; I want to be of use."

"Love!" said the big dog. "Did you ever smell it?"

"No," said Towser.

"Or see anybody eat it?"

"No."

"Or sleep on it?"

"No."

"Then what use is it?" said the big dog; and he went away.

Shortly after that Towser got up off the stone, and took his little tail out of the mud. He shook his little ears and let the two drops run off his nose.

"I'll go and seek for someone that needs me," said Towser; and so he started on his travels.

## II—His Search

"I must look as pleasant as I can," said Towser, as he went down the street; and he perked up his little ears. He really was a pretty terrier, with long silky hair. Presently he saw a boy walking on the pavement. He was ragged, he looked as if he hadn't had any dinner or breakfast either. Towser's heart ached for him. He looked very lonely.

"I'm sure he would like a nice little dog like me to be a companion to him," said Towser. "Yes, he wants me; I won't trouble him for food, because everyone gives me something when I go to the back doors, because of my big eyes."

So Towser began dancing a little dance of affection, shaking his ears and looking from under them with his round eyes. This proceeding was meant to say, "I want to love you."

"Doggy, Doggy, Doggy!" said the little solitary boy, standing still and holding out his fingers; "Doggy, Doggy, Doggy."

So Towser came close up, just curling into a ball with excitement. He didn't know whether he should lick the little boy's hands first or his feet.

"There!" said the little boy. He gave Towser a powerful kick on the tip of his black nose.

When he looked back, Towser was standing quite still, with a great singing in his ears. Then the little lonely boy laughed.

When the singing had left off, Towser trotted away down the street. He wasn't so ready to caper now. He saw several little lonely boys as he passed, but he didn't think they wanted him.

At last he got to the outskirts of the town. There was a bonny little house with roses and creepers all round. He went to the back door and put his forefeet on the step, and looked in to see if there was anybody wanted him. A lady lay on a sofa in one corner; she had not walked for ten years, and her eyes were heavy with pain.

"Dear little creature, where do you come from?" she said.

Towser made a motion with his fore-feet, to explain that he would come in if he were invited.

The lady said, "Come in," and he sat down on the rug before her and the lady felt his ears.

"Beautiful ears," she said, "come!"

Towser jumped up on to the sofa beside her.

"I never saw such large eyes," said the lady. "Dear little dog, if I can I shall keep you for my own," and she made a place for him on her chest.

He lay with his paw close to her chin, and looked as loving as he could.

Presently he licked her chin, and she said he had a soft little tongue. When her lunch came she fed him with brandy and egg out of a spoon. He didn't like it, it burnt his throat, but he drank it.

"She wants me awfully, I can just see that," said Towser, "and I'll stay with her as long as I live."

The lady had him taken to her bedroom that night, and a nice little rug laid for him across the foot of her bed. In the night, when she woke to cough, he walked up to her face and licked it, and she covered him with the blankets till there was just the tip of his black nose sticking out.

"The big, comfortable dog said love was nothing, but it's something," said Towser, "and it's nice "; and he put his little muzzle against her cheek. Next day he danced before her, and tried to catch his tail when she looked sad.

"Oh, I'm a dear, nice, happy little dog; she does love me so. She couldn't live without me; I'm such a comfort to her," said Towser. He wished he'd been six months younger, then he'd have six months more to live.

So weeks passed.

One afternoon a lady came in.

"I've brought Nola home," she said, "so much better for her change to the sea-side; here she is." And the lady put down on the floor the most snow-white terrier (Towser was brown), all soft with curls, and with little sleepy eyes.

"She looks better," said the lady—"dear Nola."

Nola climbed quietly up on the sofa and curled herself up in a little nest and shut her eyes.

Towser stood looking on. He thought he would jump on the sofa, too.

"Down, Towser, down!" said the lady.

Then Towser went and got behind the crimson curtain, with only his nose and two bright eyes peeping out. At last tea-time came, and there was a dish of milk put down on the floor. Nola got off the sofa and went to drink some; Towser came out, and put his little black muzzle in too. As soon as the curly white one saw it, she lifted her pink nose, and got quietly back on the sofa.

"Nola won't drink with Towser," said the lady; "take him to the kitchen and give him a nice basin of milk with plenty of cream on it."

Then Nola got off the sofa again; but Towser wouldn't go to the kitchen. He got behind the curtain and looked out with his great saucers of eyes.

"It'll be bed-time soon, and I am sure she is wanting me badly to lick her chin. I'm sure she is wishing it was bed-time," said Towser.

"Make a comfortable bed for Towser in the kitchen, and be sure it's nice and soft," said the lady.

Towser wouldn't get into the bed; he sat on the stone looking at the fire. He wondered if a coal had got into his heart. He felt so wicked.

"I wonder what is the matter with Towser," said the lady the next day; "he used to be such a nice little dog, always so lively."

Then Towser got up, and began dancing about after his tail, and then he got on the sofa, and began playing with the lady's fingers and rings. Then the white curly one opened her eyes slowly and got off the sofa.

"Nola, Nola, come here! Down, Towser, down!" said the lady.

Then Towser went out in the garden and sat in the gravelled path looking up at the sun. I don't know how he felt.

"Towser's such a nice little dog" said the lady one day; "quite the nicest little dog I've ever seen. I wish I could get someone to take him away; someone who would be kind to him."

Now Towser, didn't wait to be given away to a very kind person. I fancy he had a pain at his heart. He put his tail close between his hind legs, and went out at the back door.

### III—His Reward

Towser sat alone in a wood. He leaned his head on a stone at his side. He was thinking; you could see that by his big, round eyes.

"I made somebody happy, that's a great comfort," said he (for all that there were tears running down his nose). "I must be happy; I must think I once made somebody happy" —here his little chest swelled out immensely. "It doesn't matter if you're not loved if only you've made somebody happy. Yes, I won't want to be loved any more, I'll just try to help people, and then I'll be happy too. You mustn't want to be loved; just to be good."

So he took his head off the stone and went trotting away through the wood. Presently he saw a country boy before him carrying a flitch of bacon; not long after from the bushes at the path-side burst a gipsy-looking fellow.

After a minute, the rough fellow said to the boy, "Give me your bacon."

Said the boy, "No."

The man said, "I can make you; there is nobody near."

He took hold of the bacon; the boy began to struggle. He knelt upon the boy. Then every hair upon Towser's little body stood on end, and his tail was stiffened out. He forgot he was Towser, he forgot he wanted to be loved, he forgot everything, and flew at the trousers of the gipsy man. Then the gipsy man thought there was someone coming, ran away, and left the boy and the bacon.

Towser stood in the middle of the path barking furiously. He was in great excitement.

Slowly the country fellow got up; his face was purple with rage. He cut a little stick from the bush growing by; it wasn't thicker than his finger; Towser's backbone was not thicker either.

"So, you stand here barking at me, do you?" said the country fellow. "Why don't you go after your master? You want to bite me! do you? do you? do you?"

Towser thought his little backbone would be broken, and when the stick hit his little skull it was terribly sore. The country fellow held him fast with one hand; he was so small he wasn't much to hold, and beat him on his little fore-feet, and in his eye; then he took up his bacon, and walked away.

Towser went into the brushwood close by, and sat down on his tail and lifted his nose to the sky. The one eye was shut up, but the other was wide open, and the water running out of it.

If he ever went home and became a comfortable, respectable dog, I don't know; the last I saw of him he was sitting there in that wood.

*Eastbourne, March 1882.*

First published in *New College Magazine* (Eastbourne) March 1882.

# Dreams and Allegories

# A Soul's Journey—Two Visions

*"There is no light in earth or heaven,*
*But the cold white light of stars."*

A soul was born down in the deep and dark where all souls are, in a cavern under the earth. And it crept along the floor, and it saw a glow-worm and it went after it. And when it got to the door of the cave it put out its hand to take it; and the glow-worm crept into a little hole in the ground; and the soul sat down in the dark, at the door of the cavern, and cried.

And after a while it looked up, and over its head in the darkness it saw a light moving; and it got up and walked after it. And the light went on, and on, and on, and at last the soul caught it. And it sat down on the ground, and parted its finger and thumb to see what it had got. And there was a little damp matter on its finger-tips; because it was a firefly, and it had crushed it.

And the soul sat on the ground, and screamed and flung itself on the ground, and all was dark, and the soul was young. And after a while it looked up, and, in the dark on the heights above, it saw a light that burnt bright and clear. It began to climb. This light did not move. When the soul came to it, it found a house of pure gold, with windows of crystal, and through them the fierce, iridescent light burst; for the house was full of fire. And the soul walked round and round it. And it said, "This is light; this is warmth. How dark it all is elsewhere!" And it went round the house tyrol-leer-ing; tyrol-leer-ing; tyrol-leer-ing! And it went round the house and it sang. And it said, "Oh, I wish the door would open, that I might go in!" And at last it went to the door and knocked softly: and the door opened and it went in. And the door was shut behind it. And the fire burnt inside.

And afterwards the soul came out of that house of fire, with its arms above its head. And it went and lay down in the dark. And there was an odour as of burnt flesh: but the soul was quiet.

And at last the soul looked up. And above it on the height it saw a light burning, still, without flickering. And the soul stood up and began to climb. And it got to the top of the height at last and it came to the light. And the light was a tallow candle in a tin lamp and behind it was a reflector and on the lamp was written "Fame." And the soul looked at the lamp. And it went a long way off; and sat upon a rock, with its elbows on its knees. And after a while it looked up, and it saw a light burning on the height above its head. Then again it rose up and climbed. And when it had got to the top of the hill, the last range, it found the light burning. It was a great fire of logs, laid across and across; and on the logs was written "Friendship." And the steady blaze went up straight to heaven. It did not flicker or turn; it sent out a steady warmth. And the soul said, "This is truth! This is reality! For this I climbed!" And it held out its hand to the blaze. And over its head were the stars shining, but it looked at the firelight. And it went to sleep there by the fire. And at last the soul woke up. And the fire had gone out. And the soul groped among the ashes with its hands. And there was one tiny coal left; and it clung to its forefinger, and it ate the flesh away, till it had eaten to the bone. And the soul laid its hand in its breast, and it lay down on the ground by the ashes.

And the soul said, "There is now no light more. I have reached the last height. There is now no light to strive for!"

And it lay still with its face on the ground.

And after a while the soul looked up. And over its head were the stars, they that neither rise nor set: that shine not for the individual, but for the whole; they looked down on it.

\*       \*       \*       \*       \*       \*

And the soul rose to its feet.

It knew why it had climbed.

## God's Gifts to Men

The angels stood before God's throne to take down his gifts to men.
    One said, "What shall I take to the little child?"
    God said, "A long cloudless day in which there shall be no rain, to play in."
    And one said, "What shall I take to the woman?"
    And God said, "The touch of a little child upon her breast."
    And one said, "For the man?"
    God said, "He has all things, let him enjoy."
    "And what shall I take for the poet?"
    And there was silence for a little while.
    And God said, "For the poet, a long sleep in which there shall be no dream, and to which there shall be no waking: his eyes are heavy."
    And the angels went down.

*Alassio, Riviera, Italy.*

# They Heard ...

The Poet and the Thinker sought for truth.

God bent and held a hand to either.

To the poet he put out his hand from a cloudless vault of blue; the Poet saw it, and climbed.

To the Thinker God stretched his hand from the heart of a mighty cloud; the man looked up and saw it move: he mounted.

On far-off mountain sides they laboured, looking upwards.

Then he who looked into the blue, cried: "Brother, you are wrong! What lies above you is but dark cloud; reach it—you will find it cold mist. In it you will wander for ever. Over me in the blue sky is that which calls me; I rise to it!"

The Thinker answered: "Fellow, you are dazed. The sun has shone too long upon your head. What lies above you is an empty vault of blue. Enter it, you will find it empty space; you will grasp—air! Over me in that dark storm cloud lives that which calls me: when the lightning flashes and the thunder rolls and the cloud is riven, I see illuminated that which beckons. I mount to it."

The Poet cried— "Fool!"

The Thinker— "Blind!"

They both mounted.

*    *    *    *    *    *

At last, when they were very tired, they reached their mountain summits.

God bent, and took his Poet in his left hand, and his Thinker in his right, and laid them in his breast. When they awoke, they were side by side upon the heart of God. One whispered, "By the left hand, I!"; the other, "By the right!" ... and they heard the truth beat.

*Mentone, Riviera.*

# Life's Gifts

Life came to me, and she gave me a flower; and I wore it in my breast.

Life came to me, and she gave me a jewel; and I set it in a diadem and wore it in my hair.

Life came to me, and she gave me a draught of water when I was thirsty unto death; and I drank it up.

Life came to me, and shot a ray of light on me; and I did not try to catch it. I cried, "Shine on! Thou art not to be held within the hand. Thy mission is to go forward. Shine on!"

*London, 1887.*

# The Flower and the Spirit

A flower grew by the roadside.

A spirit passed.

It said: "Beautiful white flower, let me take you in my hands and carry you home. I will take you up with all the soil about you, and carry you safe."

And the flower said: "No. Your hands will disturb me. Your hot breath will curl my leaves. I grow here by the roadside in my beauty, and all look at me. Go; your hot hands will curl my roots."

So the spirit went.

And many days after it passed that way: and it was winter now, and all the ground was bare and white with frost. And the flower stood alone in the cold: and it said: "Oh, spirit, take me up, carry me home in your warm hands. I am freezing to death."

And the spirit said: "No, my hands are full with other flowers. It cannot be now. See, this is all I can do" —and it bent over the flower and wept into its frozen cup burning tears; and for a moment they melted it.

Then the spirit went its way, and the flower stood alone in the cold.

*Alassio, Italy,*
*April 2, 1887.*

# The River of Life

A soul stood on the bank of the River of Life, and it had to cross it.

And first it found a reed, and it tried to cross with it. But the reed ran into its hand at the top in fine splinters and bent when it leaned on it. Then the soul found a staff and it tried to cross with it: and the sharp end ran into the ground, and the soul tried to draw it, but it could not; and it stood in the water by its staff.

Then it got out and found a broad thick log, and it said, "With this I will cross." And it went down into the water. But the log was too buoyant, it floated, and almost drew the soul from its feet.

And the soul stood on the bank and cried: "Oh, River of Life! How am I to cross; I have tried all rods and they have failed me!"

And the River answered, "Cross me alone."

And the soul went down into the water, and it crossed.

*Amsteg, Thursday Night, May 1887.*

# The Brown Flower

The angel who guards the gates of the Kingdom of Heaven left them open one evening by chance, and a man wandered in.

As he looked at the silvery light a holy one came up to him.

"What are you doing here, friend?" it asked. "You have no pass from the Angel of Death; you must go out again."

And the man answered: "Oh, I am willing to go. I do not wish to stay here" (for the woman he loved was below and his heaven was there). "But let me only gather a few of these flowers of heaven to place on the heart of one I love."

And the angel said, "Gather them." For it knew he was in the rapture of first love, and the Angels of God look down with pitying eyes when they see soul fiercely knit to soul.

And the man gathered from their beds crimson, silver, and golden Flowers of Heaven; Rapturous-joy, Hope-in-the-future, Sweet-touch-of-hands, Union-in-daily-life; these he took and turned to go.

But the angel called him back.

"You have left the best of all," she said. "See that small brown flower growing close to the root of the tree; take that. For the flowers you have got, they are only immortal in heaven; on the earth they fade."

So he gathered the brown flower, and went.

\*     \*     \*     \*     \*     \*

And it came to pass after thirty years that Death went to visit a lonely woman who was at the end of her journey. And Death, Death the all-seeing, before whom all things are laid bare, looked into the lonely woman's bosom. Once there had been brilliant flowers laid there, by the hand of a man: Rapturous-Joy—but that had been nipped by a cruel frost; Sweet-union-in-daily-life—that she had given up to another; the Sweet-touch-of-hands—it had dropped from her while she was still young; Hope-in-the-future—it had faded and faded slowly away from her. But when Death looked into her bosom, lying against the old shrivelled breast was still one small brown flower, fresh and tender as on the day the man laid it there, and the name of the flower was Trust.

# The Two Paths

A soul met an angel and asked of him: "By which path shall I reach heaven quickest—the path of knowledge or the path of love?" The angel looked at him wonderingly and said: "Are not both paths one?"

# A Dream of Prayer

I stood on the footstool of God's throne, I, a saved soul, and I saw the prayers that rose up to heaven go up before him.

And they floated up ever in new shapes and forms. And one prayed for the life of her son, and the sufferer prayed for rest, and the wronged for redress, and the poor for food, and the rich for happiness, and the lonely for love, and the loved for faith. And amid them all I saw a prayer go up that was only this: "Give me power to forgive," and it passed like a cloud of fire.

And years passed and I stood on the footstool of God's throne again and saw the prayers go up, and all were changed: he who prayed for love prayed now for power, he who prayed for ease prayed now for strength, she who had prayed for her son prayed now for his child; but I noted one prayer that went up unchanged: "Give me power to forgive."

Again years passed and I stood on the footstool of God's throne once more, and saw the prayers go up. Then among them all I noted one I knew; it said only: *"Give me power to forgive."*

And years passed and I stood there again. And the prayers ascended, and were all changed. And I heard a prayer faint and low, which said: "Teach me to forgive." And I said, "Surely this may be granted now," for the voice grew weak.

And God said: "It is answered; even now I have sent Death with the message."

*Gersau, Switzerland.*
*May 10, 1887.*

# Workers

In a far-off world, God sent Two Spirits to work. The work he set them to do was to tunnel through a mountain. And they stood side by side and looked at it. And they began to work. They found that the place they had to work in was too narrow; their wings got interlocked. They saw they would never get through the mountain if they worked at it only from that one place.

And one spirit said to the other, "You stay here; I will go and work from the other side."

And it flew away. And they worked on, each from his side of the mountain. And after years in the dark, each one heard the sound of the other's axe, picking, and they knew they were getting near— that the other was at work.

But before they got to the centre, these spirits' sleep-time came; and God sent other spirits to take their work and place.

But they had heard each other's axes picking, in the dark; that was enough for them.

*Alassio, Riviera, Italy.*
*April 1887*

# The Cry of South Africa

GIVE back my dead!
They who by kop and fountain
First saw the light upon my rocky breast!
Give back my dead,
The sons who played upon me
When childhood's dews still rested on their heads.
Give back my dead
Whom thou hast riven from me
By arms of men loud called from earth's farthest bound
To wet my bosom with my children's blood!
Give back my dead,
The dead who grew up on me!

*Wagenaar's Kraal, Three Sisters.*
*May 9, 1900.*

# Seeds A-Growing

I sat alone on the kopje side; at my feet were the purple fig-blossoms, and the yellow dandelion flowers were closing for the night. The sun was almost sinking; above him in the west the clouds were beginning to form a band of gold. The cranes were already beginning to fly homeward in long straight lines. I leaned my head against the rock upon the kopje, and I think I slept.

Then it seemed that in the sky above me moved a great white figure, with wings outstretched.

And I called, "Who and what are you, great white Spirit?"

And the Spirit answered, "I am the Spirit of Freedom!"

And I cried, "What do you do here, in this sad land, where no freedom is?"

And he answered me, "I am watching my seeds a-sowing."

And I said, "What is there a-sowing here? Our cornfields are down-trodden; at day the flames from burning farm-houses rise into the sky, and at night the stars look down on homeless women and young children. Here the walls have ears; we look round to see if no man is following us to listen to the very beating of our hearts. What place is left for you here?"

And he said, "I have watched my seeds a-sowing. At the foot of every scaffold which rises in town or village, on every spot in the barren veld where men with hands tied and eyes blindfolded are led out to meet death, as the ropes are drawn and the foreign bullets fly, I count the blood drops a-falling; and I know that my seed is sown. I leave you now, and for a while you shall know me no more; but the day will come when I will return and gather in my harvest."

And I cried, "Great Spirit, when shall that time be?"

But his wings were spread, and it seemed they covered all the sky as he passed.

And I cried, "Spirit, beware, lest even in the sky they shoot up at you and you be killed for ever in this strange sad land."

But he cried as he fled from me, "I cannot die! ... *Mors janua vitæ!*"

And I started up. I saw no spirit, but the sun was sinking. The west was gold and crimson. The last line of cranes with their heads stretched forward and their wings outspread were flying homeward. I heard their long, strange cry.

I glanced around me on the kopje, fearing one holding by English gold might have followed me. But the kopje was silent. As I passed back into the village, the barbed-wire gates were not yet closed; only the dark-skinned guards scowled at me as I passed them with their rifles at the gate, and armed white men jeered as I went by them; but not one of them knew that I had been speaking with their great enemy on the kopje!

*Hanover, October 25, 1901.*

# The Great Heart of England

I have had a dream; again and again it comes to me, till I fear the night for its return.

I dream that in the war I have lost all my clothes. That they have shot to pieces the old dress that I wore so long and love so. And I go to have a new dress made, and I take the only stuff I can find, and the skirt is of three colours, red, white, and blue, and the body is a strip of green.

And when I have got it on I go down the street, dancing, dancing, dancing. And the people stop me and they say, "Why have you got that dress on?" And I say, "Do you not see it is the four colours? They shot all my old dresses to pieces in the war, the old dresses that I loved so. Now I could get nothing else but this." And they say, "Why are you dancing so?" And I say, "Because my heart, my heart, is broken."

And all the time, as I dance, the tune that I dance to, and the words that I sing, are the words of an old song I heard long ago when I was a child:

> "They are hanging men and women now,
> For the wearing of the Green."

And then there is a sudden stop, there is a gleam of bayonets, and a sound of guns firing; and then all is silence.

> "They are hanging men and women now,
> For the wearing of the Green."

And I wake, and the cold drops are hanging on my forehead, and I cry aloud in my anguish, "Who will save me from this nightmare? Can nothing break it?"

And then I know that one thing only can break it: if I could hear the beat of a great heart, the heart that has loved justice and hated oppression, that has sought after righteousness rather than gold,

> "That strikes as soon for a trodden foe,
> As it does for a soul-bound friend,"

—the great heart of England.

And in the dark I lean forward listening, that across six thousand miles of sea I may perchance hear that heart beat.

# Who Knocks At The Door?

I lay upon my couch. Outside for days heavy snow had fallen, and the long trails of the roses that grew over the balcony were weighted with balls of frozen snow, and the wind blew them hither and thither. They tapped upon the window panes and against the woodwork of the balcony.

I had grown weary of looking at that dreary world outside; and I rose and drew the curtains across the windows and lit the light at the head of my couch, and lay down again to read the evening newspaper.

It was the old, old story, such as one read every night: Death and destruction; "heavy losses of the enemy" —always that; and then the long straight list of names, which one followed holding oneself tight, lest one among them should stab one to the very heart; then columns of hatred and abuse; then statements which men in calm hours would never make, or balanced men listen to; omissions and suppressions, till, amid it all, the mind groped like a small animal under a pile of decaying mould seeking to find the way to one ray of light; one judged what might be truth only by what was left out, and the reality by what was denied. It was an old, old story; one read it every day. There was nothing new in it.

I was going to drop the newspaper on to the floor, and try to turn my thoughts to other matters, and then my eye caught sight of a paragraph, in very small type, at the left-hand corner on the inside page. It was printed in type so fine and the paragraph was so short that many reading might not notice it, and if they did, might not trouble to decipher it. Yet, it was something new; it seemed to have crept into the corner of the paper by chance. Having read it once, one read it over, and then again. It set one's thoughts travelling far.

Holding the paper in my hands, I think I must have fallen fast asleep, for I thought I found myself in a great forest. On every side the stems of the trees towered up above me like the aisles of some vast cathedral, and high above my head the wind struck their mighty branches together. I wrapped my mantle tight about my head and struggled on in the darkness: there was no path, and the dead branches cracked beneath my feet. It seemed to be one of those primeval forests, such as sheltered the forbears of our peoples—Suevi and Alamanni, Goth and Visigoth, Frank and Saxon, Lombard and Burgundian, before we spread ourselves out over Europe from the shores of the Atlantic and the Bay of

Biscay to Gothland, from the wet Tin Islands of the North Sea to the blue waters of the Mediterranean; who followed Ruric into the frozen steppes of the north, and Theodoric into Italy; and drank Sicilian wines with our Northmen leaders under the slopes of Mount Etna.

As I wandered in that impenetrable darkness, at last it seemed to me as though, from far off, I saw a gleam of light, and it almost seemed to me I heard distant sounds which were not those of the forest and the storm. I struggled onward, and, at last, I came to a place where through the darkness, under the over-arching trees, I could see looming a mighty building; light streamed from its windows of many-coloured glass, and from within came sounds of song and music, and loud laughter and shouts, as of those who applaud and rejoice.

I crept close up to the building, and pressed my face against a pane in a small window and looked in. It was a wonderful scene that met my eyes. Within was a vast hall built of richly carved woods, and the pillars that supported it were shaped in every lovely form, and sprang upwards into the groined roof, from which hung thousands of glittering lights; and along the walls golden torches were flaming; and beneath stood works of art, and scattered about the Hall were large tables, covered with glittering crystal and gold and silver vessels; and upon the tables were loaded all of rich and rare of viands and wines that the earth produces.

Around the tables sat men and women clad in gorgeous robes; some had golden crowns on their heads and sceptres in their hands, and others paid court to them; and the women wore jewels of gold set heavily with precious stones, till they seemed weighted with them.

And I saw that from table to table they passed the rare viands and wines, exchanging them with one another; and men and women sang and danced now before this table and then before that, and the feasters showered gold and jewels upon them; and I saw men take ornaments from their own breasts and pass them on to men at other tables. And I noticed that though there were differences between those who sat at the different tables, yet they were all really of one garb and one appearance. And I said to myself, "Surely this is some vast banqueting house, where a great kindred are holding high festival together." And I thought, "Surely never since earth was earth has so much of richness, of rarity, been gathered together in one spot." And I marvelled when I thought of the labour which had brought all these things together, where once only the trees of the forest stood.

And then, as I looked, I noticed that all the men wore daggers fastened at their sides: and as I watched, I thought I saw that though their lips were smiling sometimes their brows lowered; and I thought that some cast looks of envy as the viands passed from table to table; and it even seemed to me some whispered behind their hands as they glanced at one another: and though dance and song and feasting went on, the feeling came to me that, perhaps, all was not so well with that great company.

And then, I hardly seemed to know what happened, but at a table at the far end some drew their daggers and a man and woman fell dead upon the floor.

Then from other tables others arose and stabbed at one another, and flung one another to the earth; and more and more arose, till from end to end of that great Hall blood flowed and men fell wounded and dying to the ground. And the tables were overturned; and the rare viands and the rich wines and glittering crystals and costly ornaments and rare works of art fell scattered and broken on the ground. And I saw that, in their mad rage, men seized broken fragments from the floor and hurled them at one another, till the glass in every door and window was shattered and the very walls were indented. And I saw women, who, with wild, hoarse voices, called on the men to stab and kill yet more; and some passed on to the men fragments to hurl at one another, though they themselves fell often buried beneath the heaps of killed and wounded.

And I, looking on through the shattered window, wrung my hands and cried, "Stop it! Stop it! Can you not see, you are destroying all?" But it might have been two small leaves in the forest trees overhead clapping themselves together, for any sound the feeble words made in that vast tumult.

And in their madness I saw men drag down the great glittering lights that hung from the centre of the Hall, and fling the fragments at one another; and tear down the lighted torches that were fastened to the walls, and strike one another with them. And as the lights fell down on that seething mass that covered the floor, they set fire to the garments of the fallen, and smoke began to rise. And outside the window where I stood came the stench of burning human flesh.

And I was silent with horror; for surely never since man was man upon the earth was there such a great and horrible destruction in any Hall where a great human kindred were gathered together.

And then, as I stood gazing in, it almost seemed to me, though I could not tell surely, that, from the far end of the Hall, where the great shattered doorway stood, I heard—three, slow, clear, distinct knocks! I listened; and then again I heard the sounds, and this time I knew I was not mistaken—slow, clear, distinct! And as I looked across that fallen mass of ruin, it seemed to me, I saw, through a broken pane in the great shattered doorway at the far end, a human face looking in! The smoke came in between it and me; but I know I saw it.

And as I gazed, the flames began to creep up the walls of the Hall, and up the carved pillars, towards the roof itself.

And I wrapped my mantle tight about my head, and turned away into the darkness and the night. For my heart was *wae* for the great desolation I had seen—that men with their own hands should tear down that which with so much toil they had reared, and should consume that which with so much labour they had gathered, and that so much of the rare and beautiful should be no more! I sorrowed me over that great, brave company which had wrought so much. It might be, I knew well, that those whose knock I had heard might enter in, and take possession of that great Banquet House, and might even rebuild it in a nobler and fairer form: might build it so wide that not only one kindred but all kindreds might gather in it; and that the wine which they drank might give no madness, and the weapons be no more found at the sides of those who banqueted.

But for me, I was sore sorrowful over the destruction of that great kindred, and I wept as I stumbled onwards in the dark.

And the trees of that primeval forest, as they knocked their vast branches together over my head, cried: "*Mad*—MAD!—MAD!"

I woke: I was still lying stretched on the couch with the electric light burning at my head: the paper I had held up in my hand had fallen down on my breast. Outside the wild wind that had raged had grown silent, and the rose branches no longer tapped on the woodwork. I listened to the silence.

Then again I took up the evening paper and re-read the small paragraph at the left-hand corner on the inside page. And one's thoughts travelled far into the future.

*London, 1917.*

# The Winged Butterfly

The insects lived among the flowers. They were all soft, lovely little creatures without wings.

By and by one little caterpillar began to have tiny lumps upon his shoulders that grew out and out. "Ah," said the others, "he is ugly, see, he is deformed." And the little caterpillar hid behind the leaves, and the lumps grew more and more, and at last they came out lovely little wings. Then he came back to his fellows, and they all said, "Oh, lovely little brother. Oh, lovely brother." And he shook little wings, and he said, "It was for this I went away, for this to grow I was deformed." And he flew round. And he came to one that he loved and he said, "Come, climb with me and let us go and sit on that flower." And his comrade said, "I cannot climb; it tires me; I have no wings like you. Go alone." And he said, "No, I will go with you." And the other said, "I am going here in this little hole in the earth." And the butterfly tried to fold his wings and creep in after him, but he could not; and he almost tore his wings off in the door, but he could not. Then he went away, and he said to another, "Come, let us be companions." And the other said, "Yes, I like your wings, but you must walk by me; you must not use your wings and fly." And he said, "Yes, I will only wrap them down." And they walked a little way together. Then the other said, "You are going too fast; your wings blow you on; do go slower." And the butterfly held his little wings as still as he could. And the other said, "They stick up so; couldn't you lay them against your side?" And he said "Yes." But when he held them against his side they ached so they nearly fell off. They ached, and ached, and ached. And the other said: "What are you so slow for? I thought one with wings would go faster than another. I thought you were so beautiful when you were up in the air. You are very ugly now. What are wings for? They only draggle in the mud."

Then the little butterfly spread his wings and flew away, away, away; and he kept far from the others and flew about by himself among the flowers.

And then the others said, "See how happy he is flying about there among the flowers, he's so proud of his wings."

And one day the little butterfly sat on a rose, and died there. And the others thought it died of drinking too much honey. None of them knew that it died of a broken heart.

*Harpenden,*
*August 27, 1888.*

# The Dawn of Civilisation
(Her Last Words, in 1920)

Stray Thoughts on Peace and War. The Homely Personal Confession
of a Believer in Human Unity

## I Introduction

I have thrown these scattered thoughts, written at intervals during illness, into a somewhat personal form. I have done so intentionally, because I have felt that many persons, even those of high intellectual attainments, were not able to understand what the question of peace and war in its widest aspects meant to certain among us; that, for us, it stands for something far more intimate, personal, and of a far more organic nature than any mere intellectual conclusion – that, for some among us, as a man is compelled to feel the beating of his own heart and cannot shake himself from the consciousness of it, whether he will or no, so we are under a certain psychic compulsion to hold that view which we do hold with regard to war, and are organically unable to hold any other.

There are many ways in which a man at the present day may conscientiously object to war. His forebears may have been objectors and have handed down to him a tradition, which, from his earliest years, has impressed on him the view that war is an evil, not to be trafficked with. His ancestors may have been imprisoned and punished by the men of their own day, for holding what were then entirely new and objectionable views; but, where once a man can prove that he holds any opinions as a matter of inheritance and that they are shared by a certain number of his fellows under a recognised collective name, the bulk of human beings in his society may not agree with him, may even severely condemn him and desire to punish him; but, since the majority of human creatures accept their politics, their religion, their manners and their ideals purely as a matter of inheritance, the mass of men who differ from him are, at least, able to understand *how* he comes by his views. They do not regard him as a monstrosity and an impossibility, and are able to extend to him in some cases a certain limited tolerance; he comes by his views exactly as they come by theirs; and in so far they are able to understand him.

But a man may conscientiously object to war in quite another fashion. He may object to a definite and given war, for some definite, limited reason. He may believe that war to have been led up to by a false and mad diplomacy, to be based on a mistaken judgment of the national interests; to be even suicidal; and therefore he may feel compelled to oppose that particular war while the bulk of men and women in his society desire and approve of it. The unthinking herd, unable to understand or tolerate any opposition to the herd – will ſ the moment, may regard him as incomprehensibly wicked; but, at least, an appreciable number of intelligent persons, not sharing his view, will understand that a man may be sincerely compelled to oppose certain lines of public action which the majority of his fellows approve. They may hate him for opposing their will, they may attempt to ostracise and crush him; but, in their calmest and most reasonable moments, they do understand that they might themselves under certain circumstances be compelled to act in the same manner, and are willing, therefore, to allow him the virtue of possible sincerity, if nothing else.

But a man may object to war in another and far wider way. His objection to it may not be based on any hereditary tradition, or on the teaching of any organised society, or of any of the great historic figures of the past; and, while he may indeed object to any definite war for certain limited and material reasons, these are subordinate to the real ground on which his objection rests. He may fully recognise the difference in type between one war and another; between a war for dominance, trade expansion, glory, or the maintenance of Empire, and a war in which a class or race struggles against a power seeking permanently to crush and subject it, or in which a man fights in the land of his birth for the soil on which he first saw light, against the strangers seeking to dispossess him; but, while recognising the immeasurable difference between these types (exactly as the man who objects to private murder must recognise the wide difference between the man who stabs one who has a knife at his throat and the man who slow-poisons another to obtain a great inheritance), he is yet an objector to all war. And he is bound to object, not only to the final expression of war in the slaying of men's bodies; he is bound to object, if possible, more strongly to those ideals and aims and those institutions and methods of action which make the existence of war possible and inevitable among men.

Also, while he may most fully allow that certain immediate and definite ends may be gained by the slaughter of man by man – not merely as where Jezebel gained possession of Naboth's vineyard, for a time, by destroying him, or David acquired Uriah's wife by putting him in the forefront of battle, but aims even otherwise excusable or even laudable – he is yet compelled to hold that no immediate gain conferred by war, however great, can compensate for the evils it ultimately entails on the human race. He is therefore unable to assist not merely in the actual carnage of war, but, as far as possible, in all that leads to its success.

This is the man, often not belonging to any organised religion, not basing his conviction on the teachings of authority external to himself, whom it appears so difficult, if not impossible, for many persons, sometimes even of keen and critical intellectual gifts, to understand.

We have, in South Africa, a version of a certain well-known story. According to this, an old Boer from the backveld goes for the first time to the Zoological Gardens at Pretoria and sees there some of the, to him, new and quite unknown beasts. He stands long and solemnly before one, and looks at it intently; and then, slowly shaking his head, he turns away. "Daar *is* nie zoo'n dier nie!" ("There *is* not such a beast") he remarks calmly, as he walks away.

This story returns often to the mind at the present day, when watching the action of certain bodies of men called upon to pass judgment on the psychic conditions of their fellows, on the matter of slaughter and war. The good shopkeeper, the worthy farmer, the town councillor, the country gentleman, and dashing young military man may understand perfectly their own businesses of weighing and measuring goods, rearing cattle, levying rates, or polo playing, or the best way to cut and thrust in the slaughter of war; but, when suddenly called upon to adjudge on psychological phenomena of which they have no personal experience, they are almost compelled to come to the conclusion of the good old backveld Boer – "Daar *is* nie zoo'n dier nie!" "There *is* no such thing as a Conscientious Objector! He may stand before us; he may tell us what he feels; but we have no experience of such feelings. We know, therefore, that such a being *cannot* exist – and, therefore, it *does* not!"

In the few pages that follow I have allowed, as I said, a personal element to enter, and I have done so intentionally. As a rule, the more the personal element is eliminated in dealing with the large impersonal problems of human life, the wiser the treatment will be; and it is perhaps always painful in dealing with that to be viewed by those not in sympathy, to touch on those phases of life sacred to the individual as they never can be to any other. But I have felt that, perhaps only by a very simple statement of what one insignificant human creature has felt and does feel, it might perhaps be possible for me to make clear to some of my fellows that such a being as the universal conscientious objector to war does exist.

We are a reality! We do exist. We are as real as a bayonet with human blood and brains along its edge; we are as much a part of the Universe as coal or lead or iron; you have to count us in! You may think us fools, you may hate us, you may wish we were all dead; but it is at least something if you recognise that we are. "To understand all is to forgive all," it has been said; and it is sometimes even something more; it is to sympathise, and even to love, where we cannot yet fully agree. And therefore, perhaps, even the feeblest little attempt to make human beings understand how and why their fellows feel as they feel and are as they are, is not quite nothing.

## II Somewhere, Some Time, Some Place!

When a child, not yet nine years old, I walked out one morning along the mountain tops on which my home stood. The sun had not yet risen, and the mountain grass was heavy with dew; as I looked back I could see the marks my feet had made on the long, grassy slope behind me. I walked till I came to a place where a little stream ran, which farther on passed over the precipices into the deep valley below. Here it passed between soft, earthy banks; at one place a large slice of earth had fallen away from the bank on the other side, and it had made a little island a few feet wide with water flowing all round it. It was covered with wild mint and a weed with yellow flowers and long waving grasses. I sat down on the bank at the foot of a dwarfed olive tree, the only tree near. All the plants on the island were dark with the heavy night's dew, and the sun had not yet risen.

I had got up so early because I had been awake much in the night and could not sleep longer. My heart was heavy; my physical heart seemed to have a pain in it, as if small, sharp crystals were cutting into it. All the world seemed wrong to me. It was not only that sense of the small misunderstandings and tiny injustices of daily life, which perhaps all sensitive children feel at some time pressing down on them; but the whole Universe seemed to be weighing on me.

I had grown up in a land where wars were common. From my earliest years I had heard of bloodshed and battles and hairbreadth escapes; I had heard them told of by those who had seen and taken part in them. In my native country dark men were killed and their lands taken from them by white men armed with superior weapons; even near to me such things had happened. I knew also how white men fought white men; the stronger even hanging the weaker on gallows when they did not submit; and I had seen how white men used the dark as beasts of labour, often without any thought for their good or happiness. Three times I had seen an ox striving to pull a heavily loaded wagon up a hill, the blood and foam streaming from its mouth and nostrils as it struggled, and I had seen it fall dead, under the lash. In the bush in the kloof below I had seen bush-bucks and little long-tailed monkeys that I loved so shot dead, not from any necessity but for the pleasure of killing, and the cock-o-veets and the honey-suckers and the wood-doves that made the bush so beautiful to me. And sometimes I had seen bands of convicts going past to work on the roads, and had heard the chains clanking which went round their waists and passed between their legs to the irons on their feet; I had seen the terrible look in their eyes of a wild creature, when every man's hand is against it, and no one loves it, and it only hates and fears. I had got up early in the morning to drop small bits of tobacco at the roadside, hoping they would find them and pick them up. I had wanted to say to them, "Someone loves you"; but the man with the gun was always there. Once I had seen a pack of dogs set on by men to attack a strange dog, which had come among them and had done no harm to anyone. I had watched it torn to pieces, though I had done all I could to save it. Why did everyone press on everyone and try to make them do what they wanted? Why did the strong always crush the weak? Why did we hate and kill and torture? Why was it all as it was? Why had the world ever been made? Why, oh why, had I ever been born?

The little sharp crystals seemed to cut deeper into my heart.

And then, as I sat looking at that little, damp, dark island, the sun began to rise. It shot its light across the long, grassy slopes of the mountains and struck the little mound of earth in the water. All the leaves and flowers and grasses on it turned bright gold, and the dewdrops hanging from them were like diamonds;

and the water in the stream glinted as it ran. And, as I looked at that almost intolerable beauty, a curious feeling came over me. It was not what I *thought* put into exact words, but I seemed to *see* a world in which creatures no more hated and crushed, in which the strong helped the weak, and men understood each other, and forgave each other, and did not try to crush others, but to help. I did not think of it, as something to be in a distant picture; it was there, about me, and I was in it, and a part of it. And there came to me, as I sat there, a joy such as never besides have I experienced, except perhaps once, a joy without limit.

And then, as I sat on there, the sun rose higher and higher, and shone hot on my back, and the morning light was everywhere. And slowly and slowly the vision vanished, and I began to think and question myself.

How could that glory ever really be? In a world where creature preys on creature, and man, the strongest of all, preys more than all, how could this be? And my mind went back to the dark thoughts I had in the night. In a world where the little ant-lion digs his hole in the sand and lies hidden at the bottom for the small ant to fall in and be eaten, and the leopard's eyes gleam yellow through bushes as it watches the little bush-buck coming down to the fountain to drink, and millions and millions of human beings use all they know, and their wonderful hands, to kill and press down others, what hope could there ever be? The world was as it was! And what was I? A tiny, miserable worm, a speck within a speck, an imperceptible atom, a less than a nothing! What did it matter what *I* did, how *I* lifted my hands, and how *I* cried out? The great world would roll on, and on, just as it had! What if nowhere, at no time, in no place, was there anything else?

The band about my heart seemed to grow tighter and tighter. A helpless, tiny, miserable worm! Could I prevent one man from torturing an animal that was in his power; stop one armed man from going out to kill? In my own heart, was there not bitterness, the anger against those who injured me or others, till my heart was like a burning, coal? If the world had been made so, so it was! But, why, oh why, had I ever been born? Why did the Universe exist?

And then, as I sat on there, another thought came to me; and in some form or other it has remained with me ever since, all my life. It was like this: You cannot by willing it alter the vast world outside of you; you cannot, perhaps, cut the lash from one whip; you cannot stop the march of even one armed man going out to kill; you cannot, perhaps, strike the handcuff from one chained hand; you cannot even remake your own soul so that there shall be no tendency to evil in it; the great world rolls on, and *you* cannot reshape it; but this one thing only you can do – in that one, small, minute, almost infinitesimal spot in the Universe, where your will rules, there, where alone you are as God, *strive* to make that you hunger for real! No man can prevent you there. In your own heart strive to kill out all hate, all desire to see evil come even to those who have injured you or another; what is weaker than yourself try to help; whatever is in pain or unjustly treated and cries out, say "I am here! I, little, weak, feeble, but I will do what I can for you." This is all you can do; but do it; it is not nothing! And then this feeling came to me, a feeling it is not easy to put into words, but it was like this: You also are a part of the great Universe; what you strive for something strives for; *and nothing in the Universe is quite alone*; you are moving on towards something.

And as I walked back that morning over the grass slopes, I was not sorry I was going back to the old life. I did not wish I was dead and that the Universe had never existed. I, also, had something to live for – and even if I failed to reach it utterly – somewhere, some time, some place, it was! I was not alone.

More than a generation has passed since that day, but it remains to me the most important and unforgettable of my life. In the darkest hour its light has never quite died out.

In the long years which have passed, the adult has seen much of which the young child knew nothing.

In my native land I have seen the horror of a great war. Smoke has risen from burning homesteads; women and children by thousands have been thrown into great camps to perish there; men whom I have known have been tied in chairs and executed for fighting against strangers in the land of their own birth. In the world's great cities I have seen how everywhere the upper stone grinds hard on the nether, and men and women feed upon the toil of their fellow men without any increase of spiritual beauty or joy for themselves, only a heavy congestion; while those who are fed upon grow bitter and narrow from the loss of the life that is sucked from them. Within my own soul I have perceived elements militating against all I hungered for, of which the young child knew nothing; I have watched closely the great, terrible world of public life, of politics, diplomacy, and international relations, where, as under a terrible magnifying glass, the greed, the ambition, the cruelty and falsehood of the individual soul are seen, in so hideously enlarged and wholly unrestrained a form that it might be forgiven to one who cried out to the powers that lie behind life: "Is it not possible to put out a sponge and wipe up humanity from the earth? It is stain!" I have realised that the struggle against the primitive, self-seeking instincts in human nature, whether in the individual or in the larger social organism, is a life-and-death struggle, to be renewed by the individual till death, by the race through the ages. I have tried to wear no blinkers. I have not held a veil before my eyes, that I might profess that cruelty, injustice, and mental and physical anguish were not, I have tried to look nakedly in the face those facts which make most against all hope – and yet, in the darkest hour, the consciousness which I carried back with me that morning has never wholly deserted me; even as a man who clings with one hand to a rock, though the waves pass over his head, yet knows what his hand touches.

But, in the course of the long years which have passed, something else has happened. That which was for the young child only a vision, a flash of almost blinding light, which it could hardly even to itself translate, has, in the course of a long life's experience, become a hope, which I think the cool reason can find grounds to justify, and which a growing knowledge of human nature and human life does endorse.

Somewhere, some time, some place – even on earth!

# Glossary

*Biltong*: strips of sun-dried meat.
*Boers*: now known as Afrikaners: rural colonists of predominantly Dutch and German descent, held together by their language and their Calvinist faith.
*Bushman*: indigenous Cape tribe of hunters.
*Cape Colony*: this southwestern area of South Africa had passed from Dutch to British hands, triggering the 'Great Trek' northward by Afrikaners who, in their turn, appropriated land belonging to the indigenous population.
*Free State*: an Afrikaner republic, called the 'Orange Free River State'.
*Hottentot*: indigenous race of South-West Africa, of mixed Bushman–Hamite–Bantu descent.
*Kaffir*: indigenous black South African.
*Karoo*: extensive South African plateau-land.
*kaross*: blanket, mantle or sleeveless jacket made of wild animal pelts.
*kippersol*: a small, evergreen, African tree.
*mealie-field*: field of maize;
*Mors janua vitae*: death, the portal of life.
*Natal*: another colony that had passed into British hands.
*Northern Transvaal*: an Afrikaner republic, annexed by the British in 1877.
*pugaree*: thin scarf wound round crown of a helmet and draped to protect the neck from sunburn.
*stoep*: raised platform or verandah running along the front, and sometimes the sides, of houses of Dutch architecture.
*veld* (or *veldt*): open South African pasture-land.
*velshoens*: shoe made of untanned hide, worn by settlers.
*vierkleur ribbon*: ribbon made from the flag of the Transvaal Republic.
*vis inertiae*: force of inertia.